# The Strategic Marketing Plan Audit

A Detailed Top Management Review of Every Aspect of Your Company's Marketing Strategy

Michael Baker
University of Strathclyde

*An imprint of* **PEARSON EDUCATION**

London • New York • San Francisco • Toronto • Sydney
Tokyo • Singapore • Hong Kong • Cape Town • Madrid • Paris • Milan • Munich • Amsterdam

**PEARSON EDUCATION LIMITED**
Head Office:
Edinburgh Gate
Harlow CM20 2JE
Tel: +44 (0)1279 623623
Fax: +44 (0)1279 431059

London Office:
128 Long Acre, London WC2E 9AN
Tel: +44 (0)207 447 2000
Fax: +44 (0)207 240 5771
Website: www.business-minds.com

---

First published in Great Britain in 2000

© Cambridge Strategy Publications Ltd 2000

Published in association with
Cambridge Strategy Publications Ltd
39 Cambridge Place
Cambridge CB2 1NS

The right of Michael Baker to be identified as Author
of this Work has been asserted by him in accordance
with the Copyright, Design and Patents Act 1988.

ISBN 0 273 64940 X

*British Library Cataloguing in Publication Data*
A CIP catalogue record for this book can be obtained from the British Library

All rights reserved; no part of this publication may be reproduced, stored
in a retrieval system, or transmitted in any form or by any means, electronic,
mechanical, photocopying, recording, or otherwise without either the prior
written permission of the Publishers or a licence permitting restricted copying
in the United Kingdom issued by the Copyright Licensing Agency Ltd,
90 Tottenham Court Road, London WIP 0LP. This book may not be lent,
resold, hired out or otherwise disposed of by way of trade in any form
of binding or cover than that in which it is published, without the
prior consent of the Publishers.

10 9 8 7 6 5 4 3 2 1

Typeset by Pantek Arts, Maidstone, Kent
Printed and bound in Great Britain

*The Publishers' policy is to use paper manufactured from sustainable forests.*

# The Strategic Marketing Plan Audit

# Contents

**Part 1: The Strategic Marketing Plan Audit** .................................1

Introduction .................................................................3

The Nature of Strategic Marketing Planning ..................................5

Step 1: Executive Summary ..................................................19

Step 2: Background .........................................................23

Step 3: Mission Statement ..................................................27

Step 4: Marketing Appreciation .............................................31

Step 5: Conclusions and Key Assumptions ....................................41

Step 6: Strategic Objectives ...............................................43

Step 7: Core Strategy ......................................................47

Step 8: Key Policies .......................................................51

Step 9: Administration and Control .........................................55

Step 10: Communication and Timing ..........................................57

Summary ....................................................................59

**Part 2: The Audit Process** ...............................................61

Staffing the Audit Team ....................................................63

Creating an Audit Project Plan .............................................65

Laying the Groundwork for the Audit ........................................67

Analyzing Audit Results ....................................................69

Sharing Audit Results ......................................................73

Writing Effective Audit Reports .......................................75

Dealing with Resistance to Recommendations ..........................79

Building an Ongoing Audit Program ...................................83

**Part 3: Implementing a Strategic Marketing Plan Audit:
Questions and Checklists** ...........................................85

Step 1: Executive Summary ...........................................87

Step 2: Background ..................................................89

Step 3: Mission Statement ...........................................91

Step 4: Marketing Appreciation ......................................93

Step 5: Conclusions and Key Assumptions .............................97

Step 6: Strategic Objectives ........................................99

Step 7: Core Strategy ..............................................103

Step 8: Key Policies ...............................................105

Step 9: Administration and Control .................................107

Step 10: Communication and Timing ..................................109

*Part* **1**

# THE STRATEGIC MARKETING PLAN AUDIT

This audit is structured in three parts. Part 1 examines the process of carrying out a strategic marketing plan audit. Part 2 looks at the audit process itself and provides a framework that addresses some of the logistical and process requirements of conducting an audit. Part 3 comprises a series of questions based on the steps in Part 1. The questions are designed to help you plan and implement your audit in a straightforward and practical manner.

# THE STRATEGIC MARKETING PLAN AUDIT

# INTRODUCTION

The aim of this audit is to explain how to develop an effective marketing plan and provide a step-by-step guide to evaluating its effectiveness. To achieve this aim we provide first an overview of the nature of strategic marketing planning (SMP) and explain some of the reasons it may appear not to have achieved the promise claimed for it by academics and consultants. Next, we distinguish clearly between strategic, or long-term, and tactical, or short-term, marketing plans and the importance of developing both. Based on this, we propose a ten-step procedure for developing an effective marketing plan.

Having identified the ten key stages in developing a marketing plan, as illustrated in Table 1, we examine each of these in turn to establish what is involved and how managers can assess whether or not they have completed their analysis effectively and efficiently.

## TABLE 1
## 10 KEY STAGES IN MARKETING PLANNING

**Executive Summary**

**Background**
 A short description of the company, its current markets, products and performance. The purpose, structure and content of the plan.

**Mission Statement**

**Marketing Appreciation**
 A. Macroenvironmental analysis
  - PEST (Political, Economic, Social and Technological factors)
  - Key issues
 B. Microenvironmental analysis
  - Industry/market
  - Competitors
  - Customers
 C. Self-analysis
  - SWOT analysis (Strengths, Weaknesses, Opportunities and Threats)

**Conclusions and Key Assumptions**

**Strategic Objectives**

**Core Strategy**

**Key Policies**
 Product
 Price
 Place
 Promotion

**Administration and Control**

**Communication and Timing**

# The Nature of Strategic Marketing Planning

In his contribution to the *Encyclopedia of Marketing* (1995) the UK's leading expert on the subject of marketing planning, Professor Malcolm McDonald, observes:

"The overall purpose of marketing planning and its principal focus is the identification and creation of sustainable competitive advantage. It is a logical sequence and a series of activities leading to the setting of marketing objectives and the formulation of strategies and tactics for achieving them, together with the associated financial consequences. It is necessary because of the complexity caused by the many external and internal factors that interact to affect an organization's ability to achieve its objectives. There are two outputs from the process of marketing planning:

1. The strategic marketing plan, which covers a period of between three and five years.

2. The tactical marketing plan, which is the detailed scheduling and costing out of the specific actions necessary to achieve the first year's objectives in the strategic marketing plan.

The strategic marketing plan is a model of a unit's position in its market relative to competitors and contains a definition of market needs, the objectives to be achieved, the strategies to achieve the objectives and the resources required to achieve the desired results."

Strategic marketing planning (SMP) presents the manager with a major challenge, as it calls for a delicate balance between short-term efficiency and long-term effectiveness. Ideally the two should not be in conflict but, in an increasingly competitive global marketplace characterized by rapid change, they often are. Paradoxically, our current actions are the result of past decisions reflecting our judgment at the time of what would be best for us and our organization. If the outcome of these decisions is falling short of our expectations then, clearly, the issue is: What can we do to improve the situation? In other words, we need to think again and develop a new plan.

Effective planning requires management to address three fundamental questions:

1. Where are we now?

2. Where do we want to go?

3. How do we get there?

To these must be added a fourth question:

4. How will we know if we've arrived?

Our objective in this audit is to provide answers to these questions.

However, before examining the ten key steps proposed in Table 1, it is important to address three issues.

- What is SMP?

- How do we set about it?

- Are there any key principles we can apply?

**What Is SMP?**

As noted in *Marketing Strategy and Management* (Baker, 1991), there is no single, universally accepted definition of SMP. Seven definitions identified by Brownlie (1983) in a survey of the subject indicate its scope:

- The answers to two questions implicit in Drucker's early conceptualization of an organization's strategy: "What is our business? And what should it be?"

- Chandler defined strategy as: "the determination of the basic long-term goals and objectives of an enterprise, and the adoption of courses of action and the allocation of resources necessary for carrying out these goals."

- Andrews' definition of strategy combines the ideas of Drucker and Chandler: "Strategy is the pattern of objectives, purposes or goals and plans for achieving these goals, stated in such a way as to define what business the company is in or is to be in and the kind of company it is or is to be."

- Hofer and Schendel define an organization's strategy as: "the fundamental pattern of present and planned resource deployments and environmental interactions that indicates how the organization will achieve its objectives."

- According to Abell, strategic planning involves: "the management of any business unit in the dual tasks of anticipating and responding to changes which affect the marketplace for their products."

# THE STRATEGIC MARKETING PLAN AUDIT

- In 1979, Derek Wynne-Jones, head of the planning and strategy division of PA Consultants, claimed strategic planning: "embraced the overall objective of an organization in defining its strategy and preparing and subsequently implementing its detailed plans."

- Christopher Lorenz, late editor of the *Financial Times*' management page, considered strategic planning to be: "the process by which top and senior executives decide, direct, delegate and control the generation and allocation of resources within a company."

While these definitions differ in the particular, there does appear to be a common thread: SMP is concerned with establishing the goal or purpose of an organization and the means chosen for achieving that goal.

Perhaps the differences of opinion revolve around how one defines an organization or 'business'. Differences of size, scale, diversity, complexity, etc. will inevitably result in significant differences between organizations and so make generalizations about them difficult if not impossible. To overcome or reduce this difficulty, most analysts now prefer to define the business in terms of its strategic functions, rather than trying to define businesses first and then discover major discrepancies in strategic functions between them. As a consequence, most discussions of SMP now focus on the concept of the strategic business unit (SBU), defined succinctly by Arthur D. Little as:

"A Strategic Business Unit — or Strategy Center — is a business area with an external marketplace for goods and services, for which management can determine objectives and execute strategies independent of other business areas. It is a business that could probably stand alone if divested. Strategic Business Units are the 'natural' or homogeneous business of a corporation."

Arthur D. Little's reference to the "divestment" of a business provides an important clue to the approach followed by most major management texts. Unless targeted at small to medium-sized enterprises (SMEs), books dealing with strategy and planning almost invariably assume they are dealing with a multinational corporation competing globally through a portfolio of divisions (SBUs), each addressing a distinct market. In reality, in most advanced economies over 90 percent of the employed population are in SMEs with fewer than 200 employees. They work for an SBU!

So the formulation of strategy and the development of action plans are relevant to all sizes and types of organization. Obviously, large multinational and multidivisional firms such as General Motors, IBM or Unilever will face much greater complexity than small firms with a single product line serving a local or regional market. In crafting a strategy and putting it into practice, complex organizations will need to perform much more elaborate evaluations than will simple ones. Nonetheless, the same approach and procedures apply to all.

# The Strategic Marketing Plan Audit

During the last 50 years, attitudes towards strategy planning have gradually evolved from closely prescribed, centrally controlled systems planning approaches to much more open-ended, broadly based methods involving wide participation. In the process, much criticism has been leveled at the value of SMP. Perhaps the most influential critic has been Henry Mintzberg, who views strategies as "emerging" as managers react to events and contingencies confronting them. Few practicing managers would disagree about a great deal of strategy being formulated in this way, but most would deny this negates the relevance or importance of formal strategic planning of the kind advocated here. Briefly put, if you have no formal strategy and plans for achieving it, how can you be aware whether changing conditions call for a change in direction or know what to do next?

**How Do We Set about It?**

In developing a framework for the execution of SMP, it will be helpful to conceive of it as a process consisting of a number of discrete steps and governed by a number of specific principles.

The actual number of steps proposed in the SMP process varies. However, closer inspection of the alternative models reveals a high degree of consistency between them, as will become evident in our review of some of the better-known statements.

The most broadly based models distinguish only three stages or 'cycles' in the process of SMP, summarized as:

- Evaluation

- Strategy formulation

- Detailed planning.

Abell and Hammond, in *Strategic Marketing Planning* (1979), elaborate on this basic framework and state a strategic market plan may be thought of as involving four sets of related decisions:

*Defining the business, i.e. answering the question: "What business am I in?"*

The definition must state:

- Product and market scope: in particular, which customers are to be served, which customer functions (needs) are to be satisfied and what ways ('technologies') are to be used to satisfy the functions.

- Product and market segmentation: in particular, whether and how the firm recognizes differences among customers in terms of their needs and the ways they are satisfied.

*Determining the mission (or role) of the business—the set of objectives to be pursued*

These should be stated in terms of performance expectations with regard to sales growth, market share, return on investment, net income and cash for each distinct product/market and must be based on a full analysis of the firm's strengths and weaknesses, and the opportunities and threats facing it (i.e. a SWOT analysis).

*Formulating functional strategies, including marketing, production, etc.*

This involves interaction with general management. The results of the strategy formulation process should be completed strategy statements possessing the following characteristics:

- They should describe each of the main components of the organization's strategy, i.e. plan scope, distinctive competences, growth vector, competitive advantage, intended synergy.

- They should indicate how the strategy will lead to the accomplishment of the organization's objectives.

- The strategy should be described in functional rather than physical forms.

- It should be as precise as possible.

*Budgeting*

This involves resource allocation decisions and sales forecasts.

Abell and Hammond also distinguished the SMP from a marketing plan (MP) by stressing the latter is seen as dealing "primarily with the delineation of target segments and the product, communication, channel and pricing policies for reaching and servicing those segments — the so-called marketing mix", while the former is "a plan of all aspects of an organization's strategy in the marketplace". The essential difference is one of detail. The SMP is more disaggregated than the MP and is concerned with long-term issues. The SMP states clearly who does what, when and with what resources.

# THE STRATEGIC MARKETING PLAN AUDIT

A number of other writers and commentators suggest SMP, like corporate strategy formulation, should be the result of answers to a self-examination catechism comprising seven questions. Taylor summarizes these as follows:

1. What are the objectives to be achieved and how should we define the scope of our business?

2. What limits are set on these objectives by our personal values and social responsibilities?

3. On which strengths can we build and what are the weaknesses we need to compensate for?

4. What opportunities are to be taken advantage of and what threats should be avoided?

5. What are the main decisions to be taken and to what major courses of action must we commit ourselves?

6. What resources will be required and where will these resources come from?

7. What are the risks in this strategy and what contingency plans are required?

McDonald, in *Marketing Plans*, also specifies a seven-step sequence, as follows:

1. Defining the business.

2. Situation audit and statement.

3. Establishing objectives.

4. Identifying strategic alternatives.

5. Selection of specific courses of action ("strategies").

6. Implementation.

7. Measurement, feedback and control.

There is therefore a high degree of consensus on the basic steps in the SMP process and variations in the number of stages are largely the result of elaboration of the basic framework.

# THE STRATEGIC MARKETING PLAN AUDIT

In this discussion we have referred to 'steps' in the marketing planning process. In practice it is more realistic to think of SMP as a cyclical activity, as illustrated in Figure 1. Such a cycle recognizes that the great majority of companies already exist and so may be at any point in the cycle.

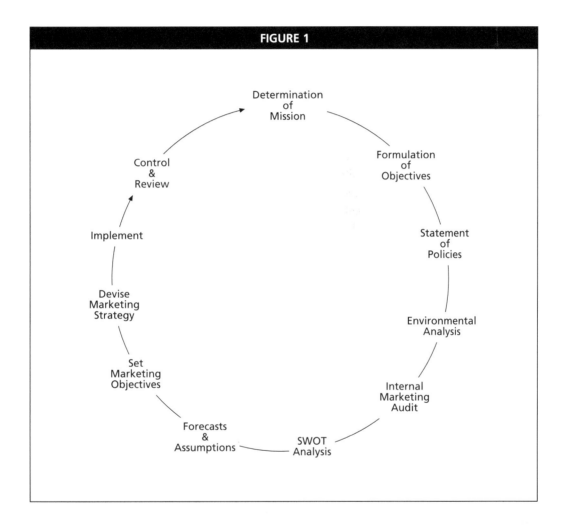

So much for the process, what about the principles governing it? One of the best developed and comprehensive schemes comes from Arthur D. Little (ADL).

# The Strategic Marketing Plan Audit

**Principles of SMP**

ADL's strategic planning process centers on five principles:

- Strategic business units or 'strategy centers' should be defined.

- Planning is a data-based activity.

- Business is not random, it is shaped by competitive economics.

- There is a finite set of available strategies for each business unit.

- Strategy selection should be condition driven not ambition driven.

All major writers on the subject now use SBUs as the basic building block for SMP.

The second principle, that 'planning is a data-based activity', also enjoys universal acceptance although, when dealing with marketing research, most agree that facts can only provide a basis for decision making. Where facts are not available or uncertainty exists about their accuracy, reliability or validity, it will be necessary to combine hard data with judgment. One should always seek to establish and secure the available facts about the environment in general, about the industry in which the firm operates and about the SBU itself and analysis of data should correspond to these three levels. According to ADL this should comprise:

- At the market level: an assessment of market size, growth and segmentation in the light of macro forces.

- At the industry level: a strategic segmentation and competitive analysis as a function of industry structure and dynamics.

- At the business unit level: an evaluation of operations, performance vs past strategies, and the determination of key strategic issues.

The third principle of business not being random predicates discernible patterns to both competition and performance. Much of the discipline of economics is founded on an acceptance of the first proposition and an understanding of market structure, conduct and performance and the insights they can provide in the formulation and execution of marketing strategy. ADL argues there are two key factors to examine in determining the strategic condition of a given business—industry maturity and competitive position.

Industry maturity is specified in terms of an industry lifecycle as being in an embryonic, growth, mature or ageing state as determined "by a number of factors including:

- Growth rate/potential.

- Product line breadth/activity.

- Competitors' number/structure.

- Customer loyalty.

- Market-share distribution/stability.

- Ease of entry.

- Technology focus/stability.

Industry maturity has implications for the natural strategies available. In addition, this concept of stages in the lifecycle also has significant implications for likely performance and cash-generation levels as well as for the most appropriate type of management system.

A firm's competitive position is determined by the geographic scope of the industry and the strategic segments (i.e. specific product-market combinations) in which the SBU is competing. Competitive position is more than just market share and is determined by a combination of three factors:

- Market share = the result of past strengths and weaknesses.

- Competitive economics.

- Other factors usually reflecting present strengths and weaknesses, e.g. technology.

The significance of market share as an indicator of a firm's competitive standing tends to increase with industry maturity.

ADL has developed its own scheme for classifying a firm's competitive position and recognizes five categories of positions, as follows:

- Dominant: Very rare and usually the result of a quasi-monopoly or strongly protected technological leadership, e.g. De Beers in diamonds, Xerox (originally) in photocopying.

# The Strategic Marketing Plan Audit

- Strong: Strong competitors can usually follow strategies of their choice, irrespective of their competitors' moves.

- Favorable: When industries are fragmented, with no competitor clearly standing out, the leaders tend to be in a favorable position.

- Tenable: Cases where profitability can be sustained through specialization.

- Weak: Either too small to compete effectively or big and inefficient.

By combining maturity and competitive position, one obtains a "strategic condition" matrix, as depicted in Figure 2.

**FIGURE 2**

|  | STAGES OF INDUSTRY MATURITY | | | |
|---|---|---|---|---|
| COMPETITIVE POSITION | EMBRYONIC | GROWTH | MATURE | AGEING |
| DOMINANT |  |  |  |  |
| STRONG |  |  |  |  |
| FAVOURABLE |  |  |  |  |
| TENABLE |  |  |  |  |
| WEAK |  |  |  |  |

# THE STRATEGIC MARKETING PLAN AUDIT

Once SBUs have been diagnosed they can be located on the matrix and appropriate strategies for them evaluated, bearing in mind the fourth principle of a finite set of available strategies for each business unit. ADL proposes six generic strategy groups:

- Market strategies (domestic and international).

- Product strategies.

- Technology strategies.

- Operations strategies.

- Management and systems strategies.

- Retrenchment strategies.

In developing strategies the final principle has to be applied: strategy selection should be driven by the condition of the business, not the ambition of its managers. This is clearly a plea for realism in selecting strategies which do not overreach the organization's capabilities or resources.

While firms at the early stages of corporate development will only have one SBU and so can move to detailed planning and implementation for the SBU, larger and more complex firms will have to undertake an additional step, to ensure individual SBU strategies are internally consistent and mutually reinforcing and so conducive to the elusive phenomenon of synergy (the 2 + 2 = 5 concept) in an overall corporate strategy.

## Developing Marketing Plans

By now it should be clear an organization needs two marketing plans—one strategic, the other tactical. The strategic marketing plan typically covers a period of three or more years and represents management's views and best judgement on where the organization is headed (its mission), what it hopes to achieve (objectives), and the broad means of carrying out its plan (policies).

The tactical marketing plan invariably covers a period of one year and is closely linked to the organization's financial reporting requirements. The tactical marketing plan is concerned with the implementation and delivery of the current version of the strategic marketing plan.

While the strategic plan will be subject to continuous revision and updating to reflect changes in the environment and competition, the tactical plan will be much more highly structured and provide for little flexibility except within predetermined

# The Strategic Marketing Plan Audit

guidelines. While strategic plans contain measurable and quantified objectives and performance indicators, these are usually broadly based and less precise than those contained in the tactical plan. If the strategic plan is a sketch, the tactical plan is a blueprint providing a foundation for operational budgets. The latter therefore needs to be clear cut, explicit, factual and formal, so those responsible for implementation know exactly what is expected and required of them.

Since this portfolio contains audits of many of the functions and activities contained within the marketing plan, this audit will concentrate more on strategic factors than on tactical ones. In doing so, it will provide senior management with guidelines for judging the overall effectiveness of the marketing plan. Providing this assessment is satisfactory, no further action will be called for. However, if it is unsatisfactory, more detailed inquiry beyond the scope of this audit will be needed. Even so, a properly prepared tactical marketing plan should contain within it performance indicators for monitoring outcomes, e.g. explicit assumptions, targets, variances, etc. In other words, if your diagnosis based on this audit calls for a deeper inquiry, the means should be built in to the existing plan.

## Setting up the Audit Team

The American Management Association Report 32 on The Marketing Audit suggests six alternative sources of audit:

- Self-audit

- Audit-from-across—persons in related activities on the same functional level audit one another.

- Audit-from-above

- Company auditing office

- Company task-force audit—a team is appointed on an ad hoc basis from within the company's staff.

- Outside audit

In practice, a composite approach would appear to be best. Effective managers invariably monitor their own performance against objectives on an ongoing basis, while formal appraisal from above will occur at least annually.

However, important as such individual auditing may be, it is unlikely to give the overall, holistic evaluation called for when assessing marketing strategy. For this reason our own preference is for the task-force approach which involves several persons with appropriate knowledge and experience and a specific remit to judge actual against intended performance. From time to time it will also be useful to invite outsiders to give an external, and possibly more objective, opinion.

With regard to the "appropriate knowledge and experience" called for in members appointed to an internal task force this will obviously vary according to circumstances. As with a financial audit, the team needs to be led by a senior manager with the authority to acquire all the necessary information and with access to the Board to ensure the audit findings will be considered and acted upon. Such a manager may be drawn from any of the functional areas within the business and there may be merit in favoring a function other than marketing to ensure greater objectivity.

Given that the marketing strategy at the SBU level is the same as the corporate strategy, and so will determine the overall performance of the business, the audit team should contain representatives from the main functions—operations, finance, marketing, HRM—to ensure the holistic appraisal advocated above. These functional representatives need to be of sufficient seniority to have a strategic point of view but may be supported or shadowed by younger and less experienced personnel directly involved in implementation.

Like the financial audit, there is a need for both continuous monitoring and a comprehensive review on at least an annual basis. The former may focus on an aspect of the strategic plan, while the latter is required to assess its overall effectiveness as a primary input to the formulation of the next year's annual plan.

As with all aspects of management, the above comments are useful generalizations which may not suit the particular circumstances facing an organization. In the final analysis, what matters is to choose a structure and procedures which meet your own needs.

*Step* **1**

# EXECUTIVE SUMMARY

While this appears first in the marketing plan, it is in fact the last stage in its preparation. With the recent developments in information technology the potential for information overload has grown alarmingly and most managers are having to become increasingly selective in terms of what they read. For this reason alone it is essential for any complex document to be prefaced with a clear and concise summary of the key issues it contains. While executive summaries are generally prepared for managers who are not directly concerned with the subject of a report, either as a specialist or as someone responsible for the detailed implementation of its findings, one should not overlook their value in providing an overview to help guide more detailed analysis.

Writing executive summaries demands the exercise of considerable judgment. On the one hand they must not be too long or else they will fail to be concise, while if they are too short they may be discarded as superficial and lacking in conviction. To some extent these conflicting requirements can be reconciled through judicious cross-referencing, so those requiring substantiation of a point or argument can turn to the appropriate section in the main body of the report. For example: "It is unlikely that any new sources or raw materials can be brought on stream within the next 5 years so costs may be anticipated to increase by 5% per annum over the period, net of inflation (para. 53.1.1-3.42)."

In essence, the executive summary is a synopsis of the whole plan. Depending on the importance and complexity of the plan, it may be anything from a few paragraphs to several pages in length. Above all else, it must be clear, logical, well structured, informative and easy to read. Like the introduction to any document, it must capture the readers' attention and make it clear precisely what benefits they will gain by reading it. Your executive summary should generate enthusiasm and conviction—this is something we want to do, this is worth doing, and we have a high probability of success.

Remember, marketing plans are written for SBUs. If you are part of a large multidivisional organization, the senior management/board of directors may well have to appraise several or even dozens of plans, all of which are competing for support and a place in the sun. Conversely, if you are a small organization with ambitions to grow, you will need to convince bankers, support agencies, venture capitalists, etc. to support what you propose. It is a cliché, but true: "You only have one chance to make a first impression." The executive summary is your chance.

# The Strategic Marketing Plan Audit

At the very least, the executive summary must make clear:

- *What* is the plan about—the organization involved, the product/service concerned and the markets to be served? What are our objectives—volume, value, profits?

- *Who* is involved—the intended customers, key suppliers, intermediaries and competitors?

- *Why* should we be preferred—what is the source of our differential competitive advantage?

- *Where* will we compete?

- *How* will we compete—what are the essential elements of our strategy/tactics?

- *When*—what are the critical timings to adhere to?

According to the nature of your organization, you may wish to develop a checklist of your own, setting out clear and specific questions to be answered. In *The Marketing Manual* (1998) we recommend the construction of factor rating tables as a means of converting opinion and judgement into numerical measures or index numbers, which can then be easily compared with appropriate benchmarks.

To construct a factor rating table we need three pieces of information:

1. What are the critical/relevant factors?

2. What weighting do we assign to each of these, i.e. what is their relative importance?

3. How do we and our competitors score on these factors?

Table 2 is an example of a rating table for five firms competing in a market across five important dimensions—price, performance, reliability, service and delivery.

The scores for each factor and firm are usually derived from a scale asking the respondent to indicate the degree to which they agree or disagree with it, e.g.

|  | Excellent | Very Good | Good | Average | Fair | Poor | Very Poor | No Opinion |
|---|---|---|---|---|---|---|---|---|
| Firm X's performance is: | ✓ | ○ | ○ | ○ | ○ | ○ | ○ | ○ |

## THE STRATEGIC MARKETING PLAN AUDIT

| TABLE 2 A FACTOR RATING TABLE | | | | | | |
|---|---|---|---|---|---|---|
| Factor | Weighting | Firm A | Firm B | Firm C | Firm D | Firm E |
| Price | 6 | 8 | 5 | 7 | 7 | 4 |
| Performance | 8 | 7 | 8 | 6 | 7 | 9 |
| Reliability | 10 | 7 | 8 | 7 | 6 | 9 |
| Service | 9 | 7 | 9 | 8 | 6 | 9 |
| Delivery | 5 | 8 | 7 | 7 | 8 | 6 |
| Score | | 277 | 290 | 267 | 252 | 297 |
| Ranking | | 3 | 2 | 4 | 5 | 1 |

The descriptors 'Excellent' etc. are then assigned a numerical value, e.g. 7 for Excellent, 2 for Poor (0 for No Opinion) and summary scores compiled for each firm. Alternatively, as in Table 2, the respondent might simply score the firm out of 10 for each dimension.

Factor rating tables are particularly valuable in enabling decision makers to capture and structure complex data and transform judgement and opinions into "hard" scores to be compared with those of other decision makers.

### Summary

By the end of Step One the audit team will have written an executive summary which covers:

- what the plan is about

- who is involved

- what is the organization's competitive advantage

- where it will compete

- how it will compete

- what are the critical timings.

*Step* **2**

# BACKGROUND

Like the executive summary, the background statement is an essential component in positioning the whole plan in the reader's mind. It provides the context for the plan. It is a preliminary answer to the first of our basic questions: "Where are we now?" Its purpose is simple—to ensure a common point of departure. Without such agreement the logic and necessity for given courses of action may not be apparent and will lead to discord and suboptimal performance. We may both agree the objective is to reach a given destination, but if you have a different start point it is highly likely your solution will differ significantly from mine.

Within organizations, it is commonplace to assume all the members share a common understanding. But, as the records of corporate performance testify, only in successful organizations is this likely to be true. All the evidence points to a lack of common purpose and shared understanding resulting in inferior performance. Given such evidence, it would be a grave mistake to assume everyone even within an organization is agreed on its current position. If this is so, it is even less likely for those outside the organization to share a common perception of it. Therefore you must develop a clear statement of the organization's current position as a basis for determining future courses of action.

The background is of no specific length but must address a number of key questions:

1. Name of the organization.

2. When established.

3. What does it do—products and services?

4. Who are its customers?

5. How big is it—sales, market share, profits?

6. Stage of industry lifecycle—growth, competitors?

7. Who and what are the major competitors?

8. What are the major issues—political, economic, technological, etc.—facing the industry, the company?

# The Strategic Marketing Plan Audit

A good example of the kind of information called for is to be found in the information stockbrokers circulate to clients as a basis for deciding whether or not to invest in a company. For example, in the SBC Warburg Dillon Read Smaller Companies Quarterly Report for March 1998, the following business descriptions for Baynes, First Technology, Luminar and McBride illustrate short background statements.

*Baynes*

Following a recent strategic review, Baynes will focus on three main areas—distribution of packaging and industrial tools, and manufacture and specialist distribution of flow control devices, including valves. The group is predominantly UK based, but the Flow Control division also has operations in Continental Europe, US, Far East and Australia.

Industrial Tool Distribution: This division is now the clear market leader in the UK, distributing tools through a network of 31 branches. We estimate Baynes' market share is 13%, some 50% bigger than its nearest competitor. Baynes has recently completed the implementation of two National Distribution Centres (NDCs) at a cost of £8m.

Packaging Distribution: The division is the UK's largest distributor of packaging materials, operating from 40 branches (17 three years ago) under the brand "National Packaging Group". For the last three years the growth of this division has been virtually entirely organic.

Flow Control: The division distributes and manufactures a range of high technology valves and flow control equipment for use in the oil and gas, chemical, nuclear, marine and industrial gas industries worldwide. In 1996 Baynes took its first step into the important US market with the purchase of Amsco. In August 97 Baynes acquired Mooney, a specialist distributor of process control equipment with a Mid-West geographic bias. An international specialist valve distribution group was also recently acquired from Tomkins.

*First Technology*

First Technology has two divisions: Automotive Electronics which principally produces proprietary crash activated sensors to cut off the fuel supply, open centrally locked doors and non-proprietary fuel level senders and brush carriers; and Safety and Analysis which produces over 80% of the world's automotive crash test dummies. Ford, General Motors, Fiat, PSA and Renault are large customers of the group. Business with General Motors and Renault is building strongly.

# THE STRATEGIC MARKETING PLAN AUDIT

Strong revenue growth is being recorded in Automotive Electronics as business with new customers ramps up ahead of earlier expectations. This is particularly true of the non-proprietary fuel level sensing units for Delphi. Production will shortly reach 5.5m units p.a. from nothing just over 18 months ago and there is also the prospect of additional third party supply by Delphi. Management are confident of the medium to long term outlook with substantial opportunities, for example, in battery cut-offs, diesel cut-offs, brush carrier assemblies for fuel pumps and mercury replacement switch sensors.

In Safety and Analysis, revenue growth has recently accelerated after a period of relatively slow progress. This is the result of increased crash testing from manufacturers, tier 1 suppliers and independent bodies, and increased legislation (child and side impact dummies). Emerging markets such as Korea have been important, accounting for 21% of divisional 1996/97 revenues.

*Luminar*

Luminar is an owner and developer of theme bars and discos. The company was initially established in 1987 to acquire and manage nightclubs. Subsequently the group developed the Chicago Rock Café (CRC) concept which was launched in 1990 and now forms the focus of the group's development.

CRC is a hybrid restaurant/bar/disco concept. Typically Luminar will take a non-licensed premises and obtain planning permission and a late license until 1.00 am in the morning. The format of a CRC is standard in both design and features. These include two or more bars (including an island bar), a raised restaurant dining area offering mainly American and Mexican food, a dance floor area and décor centred on American and rock and pop memorabilia. The music is geared to rock and pop classics. The units are located just off the town center.

The Rhythm Room is a second format being developed by the group, once again offering a mixture of food, drink and entertainment, but with a Cuban theme and aimed at a slightly more mature market. Currently there are 3 units. Two Victorian style pubs were opened in 1996/97 under the Chelsea Brewery name, but the concept has proved less successful and these will be sold.

The company currently operates 18 discos. The strategy in this area is to add further units on an opportunistic basis where there is scope to improve returns or where they can unitize space in conjunction with a CRC.

# The Strategic Marketing Plan Audit

*McBride*

McBride is Europe's major private-label supplier of customer 'own brand' household and personal care goods. Products are manufactured and packaged in the group's own manufacturing operations in the UK, France, Belgium, Holland, Italy and Spain. Principal customers include many of the major European grocery retailers who sell product under their own name.

Product lines in the Household area include textile washing detergents, fabric conditioners, dishwashing products, hard surface cleaners, bleach, toilet cleansers, air fresheners and polishes. The personal care range covers a wide variety of different hair and body items, including wash items, deodorants, and skin and nail products.

Major businesses within the group are Robert McBride in the UK, Yplon in Belgium and France, and General Detergents in Italy. The company was floated in July 1995 and was basically formed in May 1993, when BP sold various businesses to a management buy-in team. Subsequently, the management has made various portfolio changes including acquiring a UK personal care products business, and a European private-label minor brand powder business, and selling various units in the UK and Europe. Grada Group, a household liquids specialist, is a recent Dutch acquisition. The strategy of building a private-label business across Europe is based on the view that private-label share in general would grow in packaged grocery products.

**Summary**

By the end of Step Two the audit team will have written a background statement which covers:

- the name of the organization

- when it was established

- what it does

- who its customers are

- how big it is

- what stage of industry lifecycle it is in

- who and what are its main competitors

- what are the main issues faced by the company and its industry.

*Step* 3

# MISSION STATEMENT

In recent years specialists in organizational design and development have stressed the importance of capturing and communicating the nature of the firm's mission as the 'glue' holding the organization together. As it becomes increasingly difficult to create and sustain a competitive advantage based on objective performance factors, so corporate management has come to endorse the importance of corporate culture and values and their spelling out in a formal mission statement.

Irrespective of size, all organizations have a mission, a *raison d'être* or reason for being. In small organizations the mission may be implicit but clearly understood. In large organizations it may be explicit, written down, widely communicated but less well understood. Further, while the concept is fairly clear, its definition is decidedly fuzzy. Klemm *et al.*, writing in *Long Range Planning* (1989), found there was no single definition and their survey of Times 1000 companies identified a variety of terms embracing the concept:

- mission statement

- corporate statement

- aims and values

- purpose

- principles

- objectives

- goals

- responsibilities and obligations.

Based on this analysis, Klemm *et al.* detected a hierarchy in the use of these terms, defined as follows:

• *Statement 1: The Mission*

A statement of the long-term purpose of the organization reflecting deeply held corporate views.

• *Statement 2: Strategic Objectives*

A statement of long-term strategic objectives outlining desired direction and performance in broad terms.

• *Statement 3: Quantified Planning Targets*

Objectives in the form of quantified planning targets over a specific period.

• *Statement 4: The Business Definition*

A statement outlining the scope and activities of the company in terms of industry and geographic spread.

Put another way, the mission reflects cultural norms and values—it is the organization's reason for being. By contrast, "vision" represents the current leader's interpretation of the achievement of the mission, while "strategy" is the means by which specific action plans are measured against the benchmark of the vision to establish if it is being implemented in accordance with the objectives and targets.

Obviously, the mission is highly specific to the organization and must be articulated by those currently responsible for its culture and values. Despite the difficulty of doing this without resorting to "motherhood and apple pie" or generalizing to the point of becoming meaningless, it is vital for those responsible for strategic direction to seek to capture this elusive quality and then ensure their strategies and plans are congruent with it. If they don't, failure is likely, because those responsible for implementation and delivery will be unable to buy into the strategy and plan.

It is vital for the marketing plan to conform with and contribute to achievement of the overall mission. If your firm has a formal, written mission statement, then write it down in this section. If not, you will have to develop your own and secure its endorsement by both management and employees.

# The Strategic Marketing Plan Audit

**Summary**

By the end of Step Three the audit team will have written a mission statement which covers:

- the organization's character, identity and reasons for existence

- why the organization exists and for whose benefit

- the beliefs and moral principles driving its behavior

- its norms and rules of conduct.

*Step* **4**

# MARKETING APPRECIATION

While the background statement provides an overview of the current status of the organization, this is essentially descriptive in nature and designed to provide a context for the remainder of the plan.

To answer the first of our basic planning questions—"Where am I now?"—we need to undertake a marketing appreciation. As can be seen in Table 1, this consists of three major elements: a macroenvironmental analysis, a microenvironmental analysis and a self-analysis. These three are combined into a SWOT analysis summarizing the strengths and weaknesses of the organization in relation to the opportunities and threats facing it.

### Macroenvironmental Analysis

Macroenvironmental analysis seeks to provide information about events and relationships in an organization's future environment. Environmental analysis or scanning is responsible for three main activities:

- Generation of an up-to-date database of information on the changing business scene.

- Alerting management to what is happening in the marketplace, the industry and beyond.

- Disseminating important information and analyses to key strategic decision makers and influencers within the organization.

In establishing a formal environmental analysis function, certain key criteria must be satisfied. First, environmental trends, events and issues must be reviewed on a regular and systematic basis. In order to do this, it is important for explicit criteria to be established against which to evaluate the likely impact of the monitored environmental trends. Because it is a formal activity, it should be guided by written procedures and responsibility for the implementation of these procedures must be clearly assigned. Experience indicates scanning reports, updates, forecasts and analyses have greater impact when documented in a standardized format and when such documentation is generated on a regular basis and disseminated to predetermined personnel according to a timetable.

Where environmental scanning is embedded in a corporate strategy-making unit, it is likely to be charged with responsibility for monitoring, forecasting and interpreting issues, trends and events far beyond the customer, market and competitive analyses performed by many firms as a matter of routine. It may be expected to provide a broad but penetrating view of possible future changes in the demographic, social, cultural, political, technological and economic elements of the business environment. Its purpose may be to arm the firm's strategic decision makers with information and analyses and forecasts relevant to the strategies and plans governing how the firm is to respond to a changing business environment. It should also provide a basis for questioning the assumptions underpinning the firm's strategic thinking and for generating new assumptions.

**Microenvironmental Analysis**

While the macroenvironmental analysis looks at issues affecting all organizations and determining the broad basis of competition, microenvironmental analysis is concerned with the specific factors influencing the firm's competitive strategy. It comprises three parts:

• Industry/market analysis

• Competitor analysis

• Customer analysis.

Evaluation of the industry to which the firm belongs and the markets in which it competes is captured by value chain analysis.

Value chain analysis was developed by McKinsey & Co. in the 1960s as a tool to evaluate competition based on the view of business as a system linking raw materials (supply) with customers (demand) and comprising six basic elements, as shown in Figure 3.

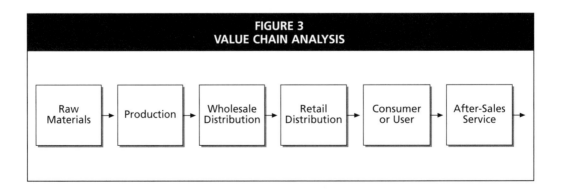

# THE STRATEGIC MARKETING PLAN AUDIT

Starting with raw material extraction, the analysis proceeds by examining each major subsystem in turn to establish the interrelationship and interdependence between them in terms of the following:

- The degree of *competition* within and between each subsystem, e.g. raw material extraction might be in the hands of only one or a few producers so conditions are oligopolistic, while retail distribution could be characterized by thousands of small sellers none of whom could influence the market. Clearly, the latter circumstances describe perfect competition, and both sets of conditions apply in the oil industry. Thus, in establishing the nature of competition one should measure:

    – the number of competitors

    – their profitability

    – their degree of integration

    – their cost structure

    – the existence and nature of any barriers to entry, e.g. technological, size of investment in production and/or marketing.

- Where, in the total system, *value is added* by the activities of members of the production, distribution, or servicing subsystems. For example, a significant proportion of turnover in many consumer-durable industries is accounted for by after-sales servicing, and the efficiency of this sector may have a radical influence on the market shares of individual suppliers, as well as on industry profitability.

- The location of *economic leverage* in the system. Does this arise from being a fully integrated producer, or can one exercise leverage by avoiding the extensive fixed investment implicit in vertical integration and concentrating on only one subsystem?

- Where is the system's *marketing leverage*? Usually this is associated with control of a scarce resource: an essential raw material, a patent on a process, control of a distribution channel, a brand name (Hoover, Elastoplast) or some other type of consumer franchise.

Once you have completed the value chain analysis, it is possible to identify firms in direct competition with you. These firms will belong to the same industry and will be selling similar products to the customers you are seeking to reach. Clearly, these firms will be the primary focus of your competitor analysis. However, you should always remember a great deal of competition is indirect. For example, in the market for consumer durables, furniture, floor coverings, white and brown goods all compete with each other for the consumer's discretionary purchasing power.

Obviously, one cannot monitor all indirect competitors but, depending on the state of the overall economy, some will offer more competition than others. For example, if the stove or washing machine break down it is likely to be replaced immediately, whereas the purchase of furnishings and floor coverings may be deferred. Table 3 summarizes some of the questions you might use to identify competitive substitutes.

### TABLE 3
### COMPETITIVE SUBSTITUTES

**CUSTOMER NEED: LIQUID FOR THE BODY**

| | |
|---|---|
| Existing: | Thirst |
| Latent: | Liquid to reduce weight |
| Incipient: | Liquid to prevent ageing |

**Industry competition**
*(How can I quench my thirst?)*

| | |
|---|---|
| Existing industries | Hard liquor |
| | Beer |
| | Wine |
| | Soft drink |
| | Milk |
| | Coffee |
| | Tea |
| | Water |
| New industry: | Mineral water |

**Product line competition**
*(What form of product do I want?)*

| | |
|---|---|
| Me-too product: | Regular cola |
| | Diet cola |
| | Lemonade |
| | Fruit-based drink |
| Improved product: | Caffeine-free cola |
| Breakthrough product: | Diet and caffeine-free cola providing full nutrition |

**Organizational competition**
*(What brand do I want?)*

| | |
|---|---|
| Type of firm: | Coca-Cola |
| | Pepsi-Cola |
| | Seven-Up |
| | Dr Pepper |
| | General Foods |
| New entrants: | Nestlé |

**Scope of business**

| | |
|---|---|
| Geographic: | Regional, national, multinational |
| Product/market: | Single v. multiproduct industry |

Once you have identified the relevant competitors, they must be evaluated in terms of the critical success factors determining performance in your industry. These vary from industry to industry: for example, for an airline access or "slots" at major airports, reservation systems and load factors are critical.

An effective competitor analysis should provide answers to the following questions:

- How are their products/services produced, distributed, serviced?

- What benefits do their products/services offer?

- How do they compare in appearance, price, performance?

- Do they have any significant strength or advantage you lack, e.g. patented technology, exclusive distribution, etc.?

- Do they have any significant weaknesses we can exploit?

- Are they growing, stable, declining?

Finally, to complete the microenvironmental analysis you should conduct a customer analysis. The essence of customer analysis is the determination of buyer behavior. It lies at the very heart of developing an effective marketing strategy.

While it is commonplace to distinguish between individual and organizational buyer behavior, they are essentially the same. In *Marketing Strategy and Management* (1992), we develop this theme at some length. The basic arguments are as follows.

Consumption is a response to a felt need prompted by in-built stimuli (physiological) or an extrinsic cue triggering a response based on experience or learning. Awareness of a need is therefore the first step in the buyer decision process. Given the number of cues or stimuli competing for our attention (awareness), we possess an in-built defense mechanism known as selective perception operating at the subconscious level and only admitting information to our conscious awareness when it is felt such information will satisfy a need.

On recognizing a cue or stimulus, we can decide whether to consider it further (interest), or ignore it—at least for the time being. If consideration stimulates genuine interest, we will evaluate both the need and the information we have about objects to satisfy the need. Given the strength of the need and the degree of risk we perceive in making a decision, we may search for additional information.

In evaluating the information we have gathered, two criteria dominate both individual and organizational buying behavior—fitness for purpose (will it satisfy the need?) and cost benefit (is it worth it?). Rationality requires us to prefer the object offering the highest perceived value. In selecting and evaluating this information, subjective influences such as attitudes, opinions and emotions will all affect the decision process.

Provided one object clearly outperforms all the others, the decision maker will have no difficulty in reaching a conclusion. The dilemma we face is, by definition, competition means we will have access to closely matched alternatives in terms of both fitness for purpose and cost benefit. In discriminating between objectively near-perfect substitutes, therefore, we will have to use our subjective preferences—what we term 'behavioral response' in our model of buyer behavior.

If this simple model of buyer behavior is correct, sellers must define carefully both the objective needs customers are seeking to satisfy as well as the subjective factors influencing or modifying the individual's perception of the objective factors. Table 4 indicates a fairly comprehensive listing of the sort of factors to be evaluated when undertaking a customer analysis.

Does your marketing plan provide answers to these questions?

**Self-Analysis**

Having completed an analysis of the external microenvironment, the penultimate step in the marketing appreciation is to complete a self-analysis or what is sometimes referred to as an internal audit. In many respects the internal audit covers the same issues as the competitor analysis, being designed to identify and evaluate assets, resources, skills and competences. But the internal audit is likely to be much more comprehensive, if for no other reason than one has open access to much more information.

In *Marketing* (1996), Baker claims the purpose of the internal audit is to develop as comprehensive a list of the organization's resources as possible, together with an assessment of their relative importance. The audit should encompass all of the following:

*Physical resources*

- Land
  - as a source of raw materials
  - as a location for manufacturing and distributive activities

- Buildings
  - general purpose or specific, i.e. designed for light engineering, assembly, storage, etc., or for heavy manufacturing requiring special foundations, services, etc.

# THE STRATEGIC MARKETING PLAN AUDIT

### TABLE 4
### CUSTOMER ANALYSIS

**WHAT . . .**
*benefits does the customer seek?*
*factors influence demand?*
*functions does the product perform for the customer?*
*are important buying criteria?*
*is the basis of comparison with other products?*
*risks does the customer perceive?*
*services do customers expect?*

**HOW . . .**
*do customers buy?*
*long does the process last?*
*do various elements of the marketing program influence customers at each stage of the process?*
*do customers use the product?*
*does the product fit into the lifestyle or operation?*
*much are they willing to spend?*
*much do they buy?*

**WHERE . . .**
*is the decision made to buy?*
*do customers seek information about the product?*
*do customers buy the product?*

**WHEN . . .**
*is the first decision to buy made?*
*is the product repurchased?*

**WHY . . .**
*do customers buy?*
*do customers choose one brand as opposed to another?*

**WHO . . .**
*are the occupants of segments?*
*buys our product and why?*
*buys our competitors' products and why?*

- Availability of and access to
  - power supplies, drainage and waste disposal
  - transportation, air, road, rail, canal, port facilities, etc.

- Plant and equipment
  - general purpose, e.g. lathe, press
  - specific, e.g. steel rolling mill, foundry, etc.

*Technical resources*

Essentially these reside in the technical expertise of the firm's employees, together with the possession of patents, licenses, or highly specialized equipment.

*Financial resources*

These comprise the liquid assets in the firm's balance sheet, the ability to secure loans against fixed assets, and the ability to raise capital in the market on the basis of past and anticipated future performance. They also include the skill of the firm's financial management.

*Purchasing resources*

Managerial expertise backed by a special advantage enjoyed by the firm by virtue of its size or connections, e.g. reciprocal trading agreements.

*Labor resources*

The skills, experience and adaptability of the workforce.

*Marketing resources*

The degree of consumer/user acceptance or "franchise" developed through past performance. Access to and degree of control over distribution and the specialized skills and experiences of personnel.

While such an audit should provide a good summary of the nature and extent of the company's assets, together with an indication of the relative importance of the main business functions, its value can only be realized by comparison with similar data for companies with which it is competing. To obtain this one must carry out an external audit as described earlier.

To summarize, the internal appraisal should provide answers to the following questions:

- What is the company's present position?

- What is the company good at?

- What are the main problems faced?

- What is the company poor at?

# THE STRATEGIC MARKETING PLAN AUDIT

- What major resources and expertise exist?

- What major resource and expertise deficiencies exist?

**SWOT Analysis**

The SWOT analysis is intended to summarize the key findings from the marketing appreciation classified as strengths and weaknesses—derived from the self-analysis and microenvironmental analysis—and opportunities and threats—derived from the macro- and microenvironmental analyses. The questions to be asked here are:

- Does the summary statement contain all the key findings from the appreciation?

- Are they classified correctly? Depending on how you look at them, many strengths are potential weaknesses and vice versa, and it is the same with threats and opportunities.

**Summary**

By the end of Step Four the audit team will have written a marketing appreciation which covers:

- the macro environment—up-to-date information on the marketplace, industry and beyond

- the micro environment—industry/market, competitor and customer analysis

- a self-analysis or internal audit—physical, technical, financial, purchasing, labor and marketing resources.

- a SWOT analysis.

## Step 5

# CONCLUSIONS AND KEY ASSUMPTIONS

This section of the plan provides the link between answering the question: "Where are we now?" and deciding: "Where do we want to go?"

The conclusions should flow naturally from the SWOT and other analyses and provide a clear answer to our first question. Inevitably, we will not have complete or perfect information, nor will we be able to predict accurately how the current analysis may be influenced or changed by future events. To establish objectives and formulate a strategy, we will need to make certain assumptions about our conclusions and how they may change in the future.

In analyzing and synthesizing data, one can distinguish three different levels— *deduction, inference* and the *formulation of assumptions*. A *deduction* is made when one derives a logically necessary conclusion about a specific case from perfect information concerning the general case. For example, all retailers of cars operate on a 15 percent gross margin; the XYZ company is a retailer of cars; deduction—the XYZ company operates on a 15 percent gross margin.

The status of an *inference* is less clear cut. An inference may be defined as the interpretation placed on evidence by an observer, so the quality of an inference may range from excellent, i.e. a very high probability of reflecting reality, to very poor. Assuming, however, the correct inference is drawn, the distinction rests in the fact there is always an element of uncertainty associated with an inference, while there is none with a deduction. However, by linking logical deductions with reasonable inferences, we can proceed a long way towards the solution of a problem.

The need for *assumptions* only arises where there is an absence of evidence necessary to link other information having a bearing on the problem. Assumptions may be of two kinds: working assumptions and critical assumptions. Working assumptions are those necessary to move an argument along and provide links in the chain of reasoning but, unlike critical assumptions, they are not vital to the final decision. In every case an assumption should only be made as a last resort, when it is obvious other information is not available. When setting out an assumption, and especially a critical assumption, it is important to state clearly the evidence considered in deriving the assumption, the reasons for selecting and rejecting particular points, and the precise form of the final assumption made. Only by careful attention to these factors will analysts be able to communicate the thought processes leading to their conclusion; without them their argument will be open to criticism and lack conviction.

Both drawing inferences and formulating assumptions demand the exercise of judgement, and this is the proper role for its application. In all other cases a strictly formal and factual approach should be followed.

The questions to be answered here are:

- Are the conclusions clear, logical and derived from the appreciation?

- Do the assumptions cover the critical issues where we lack objective data?

- Are the assumptions clearly stated and justified by reference to known facts?

This last point is particularly important because of the natural human tendency to interpret information in the light of their experience and expectations. As Hooley, Saunders and Piercy point out in *Marketing Strategy and Competitive Positioning* (1998), firms tend to force evidence to fit their preconceptions and ignore anything contradictory. Thus, in the 1960s, Cunard assumed, because the cost of transatlantic travel was so high, people would prefer a leisurely, comfortable crossing taking several days to an uncomfortable flight lasting a few hours. This incorrect assumption resulted in a massive increase in unwanted tonnage. Similarly, Xerox's assumption of its leadership in photocopying made it ignore Canon until the latter was well established as a competitor. Only then did Xerox benchmark Canon and find its assumption of technological leadership was misplaced.

### Summary

At the end of Step Five the audit team will have written conclusions and key assumptions which cover:

- where the organization is now

- where it wants to go.

# Step 6

# STRATEGIC OBJECTIVES

Pre-eminent among managerial roles is to determine courses of action which will realize the maximum potential of their resources—human, physical, financial and technological. In order to achieve this, managers must be able to identify the various possibilities (hence the SWOT analysis) and then select the strategy or course of action with the greatest promise of success. In other words, they must set objectives.

However, setting objectives is a sterile and pointless exercise unless there is also a system for monitoring their achievement. Vague and imprecise statements of the "We intend to become the biggest/best/most profitable or whatever company in our industry" kind are inadequate for this purpose. If you are not pointing in the right direction to begin with, it is highly unlikely you will arrive at the intended destination. So objectives must satisfy at least three conditions:

- They must define a precise end result.

- They must set out the conditions and assumptions on which they are based.

- They must spell out the performance indicators and timetable to be used in assessing their achievement.

For example, a specific objective satisfying these conditions might be:

"In the financial year ending on 31 December 1999 we will increase our sales of widgets by 10 percent in the domestic market having increased prices by 6 percent, to allow for the assumed rate of inflation for the period, and maintaining our marketing expenditure:sales ratio at 12 percent."

In discussing market objectives, Peter Drucker (in *The Practice of Management*, 1954) identifies seven he believes must be given explicit consideration in any company:

1. The desired standing of the existing products in their market in turnover and percentage share measured against direct and indirect competition.

2. The desired standing of existing products in new markets measured as in point 1.

3. Existing products to be phased out and ultimately abandoned, and the future product mix.

# THE STRATEGIC MARKETING PLAN AUDIT

4. New products needed in existing markets, the number, their properties and the share targets.

5. The new markets these new products will help to develop, in size and share.

6. The distribution organization needed to accomplish the marketing goals and the pricing policy appropriate to them.

7. A service objective, measuring how well customers should be supplied with what they consider value.

Implicit in this approach is the concept of a portfolio of products, possibly at quite different stages in their lifecycle, as detailed in the analytical framework proposed by the Boston Consulting Group.

McKay (*Marketing Mystique*) identifies only three basic marketing objectives—to enlarge the market, to increase market share and to improve profitability—but proceeds to spell out a number of distinct strategies for achieving them:

*To enlarge the market*

By innovation or product development:
- Through improving existing products or lines to increase use
- Through developing new products or lines.

By innovation or market development:
- Through developing present end-use markets
- Through discovering new end-use markets.

*To increase market share*

By emphasizing product development and product improvement for competitive advantage:
- Through product performance
- Through product quality
- Through product features.

By emphasizing persuasion effort for competitive advantage:
- Through sales and distribution
- Through advertising and sales promotion.

By emphasizing customer-service activities for competitive advantage:
- Through ready availability, order handling and delivery service
- Through credit and collection policies
- Through after-sales product service.

*To improve profitability*

By emphasizing sales volume for profit leverage:
- Through strengthened sales and distribution effort
- Through strengthened advertising and sales promotion effort
- Through strengthened advertising effort.

By emphasizing elimination of unprofitable activities:
- Through pruning products and lines
- Through pruning sales coverage and distribution
- Through pruning customer services.

By emphasizing price improvement:
- Through leadership in initiating needed price increases
- Through differentiating products and services from those of competitors.

By emphasizing cost reduction:
- Through improved effectiveness of marketing tools and methods in product planning, in persuasion activities and in customer service activities.

McKay also offers a series of guidelines for formulating objectives and strategies based on his own extensive review of the literature. It is worth stressing one point: "Each strategy carries with it certain essential related commitments, which must be accepted when the strategy is selected."

**Summary**

By the end of Step Six the audit team will have written strategic objectives which will:

- be clearly stated
- define a precise end result
- set out the conditions and assumptions on which they are based
- include performance indicators and the timetable for their assessment.

*Step* **7**

# CORE STRATEGY

In basic and simple terms, strategy may be seen as one of three choices—undifferentiated, differentiated and concentrated. The key characteristics of these three strategies are summarized in Table 5.

**TABLE 5
ALTERNATIVE STRATEGIES**

| STRATEGY | CHARACTERISTICS |
| --- | --- |
| Undifferentiated | • Firm has one marketing mix for the entire market.<br>• This strategy rests on the assumption of user homogeneity and/or an implicit acceptance that there is no prior ability to segment a market and so must appeal to all of it.<br>• Firms follow this strategy on the precept that what's good for the market is good for them.<br>• Such a strategy is rarely successful because markets are not homogeneous, but are made up of different types of buyers with diverse wants regarding product benefits, price, channels of distribution and service. |
| Differentiated | • This is the policy of attacking the market by tailoring separate product and marketing programs for each segment.<br>• This strategy implies an ability to segment a market and to cater for the varying needs of the different segments.<br>• Firms will tend to concentrate their efforts on selected segments which they will seek to dominate.<br>• Firms will have several marketing mixes. |
| Concentrated (focus) | • Activities are concentrated on a particular market with a view to achieving a stronger position within the market, e.g. through further investment and/or aggressive marketing.<br>• Firms will have one marketing mix.<br>• This is often the best strategy for the smaller firm. |

Your plan should have a clear statement of the core strategy to be followed, supported by a short statement justifying its selection.

# THE STRATEGIC MARKETING PLAN AUDIT

Some key questions to ask yourself in selecting a core strategy are given in Table 6. A tick (✔) in the strategy column indicates the options available to you.

### TABLE 6

|  | UNDIFFERENTIATED | DIFFERENTIATED | FOCUS |
|---|:---:|:---:|:---:|
| **Firm size:** | | | |
| Large | ✔ | ✔ | ✔ |
| Medium | | ✔ | ✔ |
| Small | | | ✔ |
| **Market share for product:** | | | |
| Large | ✔ | ✔ | ✔ |
| Medium | | ✔ | ✔ |
| Small | | | ✔ |
| **Cost structure:** | | | |
| Low | ✔ | ✔ | ✔ |
| Medium | | ✔ | ✔ |
| High | | | ✔ |
| **Access to distribution:** | | | |
| Wide (extensive) | ✔ | ✔ | ✔ |
| Average (selective) | | ✔ | ✔ |
| Low (intensive) | | | ✔ |
| **Uniqueness of product:** | | | |
| Low | ✔ | | |
| Medium | | ✔ | |
| High | ✔ | ✔ | ✔ |

Large firms with economies of scope and scale enjoy the widest choice, as they can select any one of the three core strategies. Normally, however, they will go for an undifferentiated strategy where they have a unique product with mass market appeal, such as Coca-Cola or Levi's 501s, as this will enable them to maintain their scale economies and market leadership.

If the market is segmented, as it is for most industrial and consumer durable products, the large firm will adopt a differentiated strategy and develop specific products for all market segments, e.g. General Motors, GEC. Medium-sized organizations may also be able to cater for two or more segments, in which case they will follow a differentiated strategy. However, because of their size small firms will only be able to cater for a single segment and so they will pursue a focus strategy.

**Summary**

By the end of Step Seven the audit team will have written a core strategy statement which includes justification of why the particular strategy was selected.

*Step* **8**

# KEY POLICIES

Once we have selected objectives and a core strategy ('Where do I want to go?') we must address the question: "How am I going to get there?" This question lies at the very heart of the operational marketing plan and may call for extensive detail. For example, Hiebing and Cooper's (1997) *The Successful Marketing Plan* contains 245 pages devoted to the development of a marketing mix to support the chosen strategy.

The marketing mix refers to the apportionment of effort, the combination, the designing, and the integration of the elements of marketing into a program or 'mix' which, on the basis of an appraisal of market forces, will best achieve the objectives of an enterprise at a given time.

There is a wide diversity among marketers on which elements compose the marketing mix. Some of them talk of the marketing mix in terms of the 4Ps, i.e. product, price, place and promotion. Some others add a fifth element, i.e. post-sales service, while some marketers talk about seven Ps and one A—product, price, promotion, packaging, personal selling, publicity, physical distribution and advertising. In fact, the mix elements and their relative importance may differ from industry to industry, from company to company and quite often during the life of the product itself. Furthermore, the marketing mix must take full cognizance of the major environmental dimensions of the marketplace.

In tailoring its mix, a firm will seek to offer the one target customers will see as superior to those offered by competitors. This goal of offering a marketing mix superior to competition is termed the differential advantage.

For the purposes of this audit we will consider the marketing mix in terms of the 4Ps, elaborated into a checklist as shown in Table 7.

Given the potential complexity of the marketing mix and the potential degree of detail required, we can only outline some of the key issues which should be addressed at the policy level.

| TABLE 7 COMPONENTS OF THE MARKETING MIX ||||
|---|---|---|---|
| PRODUCT | PRICE | PROMOTION | PLACE |
| Quality | List price | Advertising | Distributors |
| Features | Discounts | Personal selling | Retailers |
| Name | Allowances | Sales promotion | Locations |
| Packaging | Credit | Direct marketing | Inventory |
| Services | | Public relations | Transport |
| Guarantee | | | |

*Product Policy*

Key questions to be addressed in terms of the product include:

- At what stage in its lifecycle is the product—introduction/growth/maturity/decline?

- Is demand elastic or inelastic?

- Is the product differentiated or undifferentiated?

- Is the product pushed into the market via distributors or pulled using advertising and promotion?

- Are sales growing/stable/declining?

- Are there close substitutes for the product?

- How well does the product meet user needs—excellent/good/fair/poor?

- What proportion of sales are attributable to products launched in the last five years?

- What plans are there for new product development?

*Price Policy*

- Is there a clear statement of factors influencing pricing decisions?

- Is there a clear pricing objective(s)—what is it?

- Is explicit account taken of cost, demand and competition in developing the policy?

- Which strategy—skimming (high) or penetration (low)—are you following? Why?

- How important is price in the marketing mix as a whole?

- Is there a clear statement and justification of the method chosen?

*Distribution Policy*

- Is distribution exclusive, selective or intensive (mass)? Why?

- How long are channels of distribution?

- How many and what kinds of intermediary are involved?

- Who controls the channel?

*Promotion Policy*

- What is the promotional objective?

- How will achievement of this objective be measured?

- What do we want to tell the target audience?

- How do we intend to tell them? What vehicle or medium do we intend to use, in what proportions?

- What is the balance between personal (selling) and impersonal (advertising, sales promotion) methods?

- What measures are to be used to measure the effectiveness of the chosen methods?

Having assessed the individual policies, it is important to ask whether these are consistent with each other and adequately integrated into a coherent whole. For example, a push strategy calls for an emphasis on personal selling, a pull strategy for extensive advertising and sales promotion; high prices for exclusive distribution, low prices for intensive distribution, etc.

**Summary**

By the end of Step Eight the audit team will have written key policies which cover:

- product
- price
- distribution
- promotion.

# Step 9

# ADMINISTRATION AND CONTROL

In this section of the plan it must be set out who is to be responsible for implementing the proposals contained in it, together with a clear statement of areas of responsibility and authority. Lines of reporting and control must be spelt out, as must the type and frequency of measures to monitor performance. While separate budgets for the major mix policy areas will have been included in the discussion, the administration and control section is where they should be integrated into a complete budget for the marketing function.

While the preparation of marketing budgets is beyond the scope of this audit, in the *Encyclopedia of Marketing* (1995) Wilson suggests five questions the auditor might ask to assess the overall validity of the strategic marketing plan:

1. By how much (if any) would the net profit contribution of the most profitable products be increased if there were an increase in specific marketing outlays, and how would such a change affect the strategy of competitors in terms of, say, market shares?

2. By how much (if any) would the net losses of unprofitable products be reduced if there were some decrease in specific marketing outlays?

3. By how much (if any) would the profit contribution of profitable products be affected by a change in the marketing effort applied to the unprofitable products, and vice versa, and what would be the effect on the total marketing system?

4. By how much (if any) would the total profit contribution be improved if some marketing effort were diverted to profitable territories or customer groups from unprofitable territorial and customer segments?

5. By how much (if any) would the net profit contribution be increased if there were a change in the method of distribution to small unprofitable accounts or if these accounts were eliminated?

## Step 10

# COMMUNICATION AND TIMING

This heading is not often found in books on market planning, probably on the grounds that formal lines of reporting should be contained under the administration heading. Our reason for suggesting separate treatment stems from knowledge of business failures frequently arising from a lack of communication or miscommunication.

Lack of communication may be a simple case of someone forgetting to tell you or else wrongly assuming you already possess the information in question. Checklists of information required, written plans and formal reporting systems should overcome this deficiency. Much more serious is the situation where the information does not exist because no one has identified the need for it and taken steps to acquire it. Clearly, this is the responsibility of the marketing information system and the marketing research function, but most marketing planners make no explicit provision for spelling out a program of information gathering and dissemination. Because communication is a two-way process, it is essential for the firm to have clear policies for both gathering and disseminating information.

Everything before this in the plan represents an action plan based on past information, whereas the communication section is concerned with making good gaps in past information as well as acquiring the new data needed for future plans.

While sequences and timings will have been set out for various activities in the preceding part of the plan, this heading provides the opportunity to consolidate these into a single, comprehensive timetable.

Draw up a flowchart of the various stages of preparing the marketing plan and allocate a timescale for each one (see example on following page).

# The Strategic Marketing Plan Audit

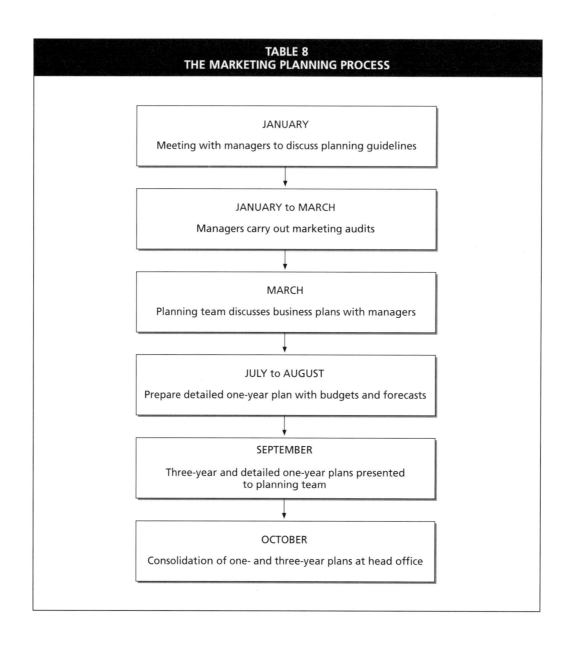

# THE STRATEGIC MARKETING PLAN AUDIT

# SUMMARY

The purpose of this Strategic Marketing Plan Audit has been to provide an overview of the factors to be covered by an effective plan, together with a series of checklists and self-assessment questions. As such, it provides guidelines for assessing the completeness and integrity of a formal plan.

While it defines the structure and desired content of a marketing plan, it is *not* a guide to preparing a marketing plan, as this calls for far more detail than can be covered in an audit of this kind.

A good plan possesses a number of characteristics. It:

- *Provides for accomplishing the mission:* Does it accomplish the objective of the planning?

- *Is based on facts and valid assumptions:* Have all pertinent data been considered? Are the data accurate? Have assumptions been reduced to a minimum?

- *Provides for the use of existing resources:* Is the plan workable? Are any resources organic to the organization not being fully utilized? Should any resources available from higher headquarters be used?

- *Provides the necessary organization:* Does the plan clearly establish relationships and fix responsibilities?

- *Provides continuity:* Does the plan provide the organization with personnel, material and arrangements for the full period of the contemplated operation?

- *Provides decentralization:* Does the plan delegate authority to the maximum extent consistent with the necessary control?

- *Provides direct contact:* Does the plan permit coordination during execution by direct contact between co-equals and counterparts at all levels?

- *Is simple:* Have all elements not essential to successful action been eliminated? Have all elements been reduced to their simplest forms? Have all possibilities for misunderstanding been eliminated?

# THE STRATEGIC MARKETING PLAN AUDIT

- *Is flexible:* Does the plan leave room for adjustment to change in operating conditions? Where necessary, are alternative courses of action stipulated?

- *Provides control:* Do adequate means exist, or have they been provided, to ensure the plan is carried out in accordance with the commander's intent?

- *Is coordinated:* Is the plan fully coordinated? When appropriate, has the commander been informed of non-concurrence or non-coordination?

If your plan gives positive answers to these questions,* it stands a strong chance of succeeding.

*(\* Reproduced from FM 101-5, 14 June 1968, by permission of The Department of the Army.)*

*Part* 2

# THE AUDIT PROCESS

This section addresses the logistical and process requirements of conducting an audit. The topics covered in this section include:

- Staffing the audit team

- Creating an audit project plan

- Laying the groundwork for the audit

- Analyzing audit results

- Sharing audit results

- Writing effective audit reports

- Dealing with resistance to audit recommendations

- Building an ongoing audit program

# STAFFING THE AUDIT TEAM

Who conducts the audit is as important in many ways as how the audit is conducted. In fact, the people selected for the audit team will, in large part, determine how the audit is done, how results are analyzed, and how findings are reported. The following list includes general characteristics of effective audit teams for most areas:

- Consists of three to four people.

- Reports to CEO or other senior executive.

- Represents a carefully selected range of skills and experience.

More than four people may be needed for an audit team if data gathering is labor intensive, as when large numbers of customers or employees must be interviewed. However, audit teams of more than six or seven people present problems of maintaining uniformity and communicating audit progress and findings during the course of the evaluation.

**Selecting an Audit Team Leader**

The audit team leader will play a strong role in shaping both the data gathering and the findings from the audit. The strength of the team leader will also influence the acceptance of the audit, both in terms of enlisting cooperation in the data gathering phase and in securing support for improvement initiatives that grow out of the audit. Because of the importance of this role, care should be taken in selecting the appropriate person for the job. The following qualities are found in successful audit team leaders:

- Has a good relationship with the CEO or with the executive-level sponsor of the audit.

- Is well-liked and well-respected at all levels of the organization, especially in the area to be audited.

- Has good interpersonal skills; can maintain good relationships even in difficult circumstances.

- Has good analytical skills; can assimilate and process large amounts of complex data quickly.

- Has some knowledge of the function or area being audited.

- Has extensive knowledge of the type of process being audited.

- Communicates ideas clearly and effectively.

**Skills to Be Represented on the Audit Team**

Once the team leader has been chosen, audit team members should be selected on the basis of what each can bring to the project. Selection efforts should focus on developing a balanced representation of the following qualities:

- A variety of tenures in the organization, with relative newcomers preferably having experience in other organizations.

- A variety of familiarity with the area (function or site) being audited. Those who are intimately familiar with the area can serve as guides to the less familiar; those who are new to the area can provide objectivity and ask questions that might never be considered by those more involved in the area.

- Considerable familiarity with the type of process being audited. For this reason, many organizations call on people filling roles in similar processes from other parts of the company to work on audit teams.

- Good analytical skills.

- Good interpersonal skills.

- Good facilitation and interviewing skills.

- Good communication skills.

- An understanding of the company's strategy and direction.

# CREATING AN AUDIT PROJECT PLAN

Creating an audit project plan accomplishes the following objectives:

- Ensures the allocation of adequate resources, or helps audit team members be prepared to improvise in the face of short resources.

- Ensures the audit is timed so resources are available that may be in high demand.

- Creates clear expectations in the minds of team members about what must be done, and when — especially important when they are not committed to the project full-time.

- Ensures accountability for what must be done, who is responsible for which tasks, and when the audit must be completed.

Financial audits often rely on the Critical Path Method (CPM) of project planning. This method was originally developed by the US Department of Defense during World War II to facilitate the timely completion of weapons development and production. It has since been modified to plan a wide variety of projects. The following outline is a simplification of CPM. It suggests the aspects of a project that should be taken into account during the planning phase.

**Critical Path Method**

In developing the project plan, audit team members should ask and answer the following questions:

- *What tasks must be performed?*

This list should include the major tasks outlined in the audits, along with subtasks that grow out of those major headings. It should also include any tasks mandated by unique circumstances in the company performing the self-assessment. The audit team may want to brainstorm about tasks that need to be performed, then refine the list to reflect the work priorities of the audit.

- *In what order will the tasks be completed?*

Answering this question should include an analysis of which tasks and sub tasks are dependent on others. Which tasks cannot begin until another has been completed? Which tasks can be done at any time? The audit team may want to place the ordered task on a time line, with start dates, expected duration of the step, and end dates outlined for each task.

- *Who will perform each task?*

Most tasks will be performed by members of the audit team. These assignments should be made by taking the strengths of each team member into consideration, as well as the time availability of each person. Equity of work load should also be taken into account. If tasks are to be assigned to people not on the audit team, those individuals should be included or consulted at this point.

- *What resources will be needed for each step?*

Each task should be analyzed in terms of the personnel, budget, equipment, facilities, support services, and any other resources that will be needed for its completion. The team should assess the availability of all of the resources. Consideration should be given to the task ordering completed earlier. Are some resources subject to competing demands, and therefore difficult to secure at a particular time? How far in advance do arrangements for resources need to be made? Does the task order or time line need to be revised in light of what is known about resource availability?

- *Where is the slack time?*

Slack time is unscheduled time between dependent tasks. Slack provides a degree of flexibility in altering the start dates of subsequent tasks. Slack time signals that a task has a range of possible start dates. It is used to determine the critical path.

- *What is the critical path?*

The critical path in a project is the set of tasks that must be completed in a sequential, chronological order. If any task on the critical path is not completed, all subsequent tasks will be delayed. Delays at any point in the critical path will result in an equivalent delay in the completion of the total project.

Regardless of the method used to develop the project plan, no project, regardless how simple, is ever completed in exact accordance with its plan. However, having a project plan allows the team to gauge its progress, anticipate problems and determine where alternative approaches are needed.

# Laying the Groundwork for the Audit

Once the team has been selected and a project plan developed, the audit leader should prepare those who will be involved in and affected by the audit for the team's visit or for data-gathering. The following steps will help the audit to run more smoothly:

**Communicate Executive Support for the Audit**

Demonstrating executive support for the audit accomplishes two goals. First, it increases the chances that those involved in the area being audited will cooperate with data gathering efforts. Second, it shows executive support for the area being audited and suggests a commitment to improving the area's performance.

In many companies, the audit is introduced by the executive sponsor of the audit by means of a memo. The memo should explain the purpose of the audit and ask for the support of everyone in the area being audited. This memo is distributed to everyone within the company who will be affected by or involved in the data gathering process. The most effective memos explain how the audit results will be used, reassuring those who will be responding to audit team requests about the motives of the audit. The credibility of such memos is also bolstered when previous audits have been acted upon with positive results.

**Make Arrangements with the Area to Be Audited**

The audit team leader should check with the appropriate manager in charge of the process or site being audited to arrange for any required on-site visits, interviewing, surveys, focus groups, or written information needed for the audit. The team leader should also explain the purpose, scope, and expected duration of the audit; review the project plan with the manager; and answer any questions the manager has about the audit.

The team leader should also work with the appropriate manager or managers to determine how the audit can be conducted with the least impact on the flow of work. This may include discussions about the timing of the audit, the options for data gathering, the availability of needed data, and possibilities for generating the necessary information quickly and easily. Finding ways to make data collection more efficient and effective is especially important when the audit is part of an ongoing program, rather than an isolated assessment.

# The Strategic Marketing Plan Audit

### Develop a Protocol or Checklist

A protocol or checklist can be used by the audit team to outline the issues that are central to the audit. Written guides can help the leaders of those areas being audited to prepare for the audit. A protocol represents a plan of what the audit team will do to accomplish the objectives of the audit. It is an important tool of the audit, since it not only serves as the audit team's guide to collecting data, but also as a record of the audit procedures completed by the team. In some cases, audit teams may even want to format the checklist in a way that allows them to record their field notes directly on the checklist.

The checklist should include no more than twenty major items, and checklists should be updated with each audit in order to ensure that the appropriate measures are taken. Items where improvement initiatives have been successful should be eliminated from the checklist, with newly identified possibilities for improvement opportunities added.

THE STRATEGIC MARKETING PLAN AUDIT

# ANALYZING AUDIT RESULTS

Discovering gaps between a company's targets and its actual performance is a relatively easy task. Tools are provided to assist audit teams in assessing their performance in a given area. In most cases, more opportunities for improvement will be uncovered by an audit than can be addressed by the resources and energy available. Therefore, one of the most difficult aspects of analyzing the results of an audit lies in determining which opportunities are the most important for managers to pursue.

Because resources and energy for pursuing improvement initiatives are limited, choices must be made about which options are most important. Sometimes these decisions are based on political winds in the company, or on what has worked well in the past, or on personal preferences of top management. However, scarce resources will be used more effectively if allocated to the areas where they will have the greatest impact. Managers must also determine the most effective way to approach initiatives. This section discusses criteria for prioritizing opportunities that grow out of audit findings.

**The Novations Strategic Alignment Model**

The mid-1980s saw the birth of the "excellence" movement, where many companies tried to achieve excellence in every area of endeavour. Although the movement created an awareness of the need for management improvements, it failed to consider that not all management processes are equal in terms of producing benefits. As a result, leading organizations in today's environment focus on performing well in a few core areas. Knowing what those core areas are depends on a clear vision of the company's strategy.

Strategic thinking about which areas should be improved involves much more than taking an inventory of current capabilities and weaknesses. If it did not, existing capabilities would always determine strategic objectives, and organizational growth and development would come to a halt. To set priorities strategically, companies must decide which improvement opportunities fall in the following categories:

- What to do themselves.

- What to do with someone else.

- What to contract others to do.

- What not to do.

# THE STRATEGIC MARKETING PLAN AUDIT

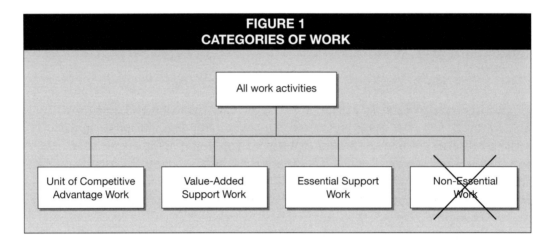

Figure 1 illustrates the four categories of work.

Unit of Competitive Advantage (UCA) Work includes work and capabilities that create distinctiveness for the business in the marketplace.

Value-added Support Work facilitates the accomplishment of the UCA work. For example, a company may have a technology orientation rather than a service orientation, but an effective logistics process may help them to improve their UCA work of providing cutting edge technology.

Essential Support Work neither creates advantage nor facilitates the work that creates advantage, but must be done if businesses are to continue to operate (includes such things as paying taxes, maintaining payroll records, etc.).

Nonessential Work is activity that has lost its usefulness but continues to be done because of tradition.

Despite their sophistication in dealing with other aspects of business, most managers have archaic views of the different types of work. Many of their models for characterizing work have come from a finance or accounting orientation. Accounting terms such as overhead, direct labor, and indirect labor may be useful as a way to report costs, but they provide little understanding about the relative strategic importance of the work. Yet these classifications are frequently used to determine how work is organized and where resources are allocated.

The concept of unit of competitive advantage (UCA) helps to explain why some organizations either emphasize the wrong capabilities or de-emphasize the right capabilities. UCA also explains why some forms of improvement lead to competitive disadvantage, and why some businesses consistently outperform their competitors by gaining greater leverage from their competitive advantages.

# The Strategic Marketing Plan Audit

A company's UCA includes the critical processes that create distinctiveness within an established strategic direction. It is based on the premise that businesses create competitive advantage when they focus their attention on a few key processes and implement those key processes in world-class fashion. For example, continuous improvement is a popular management program that assumes benefit from any kind of ongoing improvement. Generally speaking, however, continuous improvement program will only create competitive advantage when an organization defines a strategic direction, clarifies strategic objectives, and determines its UCA. These crucial prerequisites tell where continuous improvement efforts should be focused to create maximum leverage. They suggest what kinds of work to improve interdependently, what kinds to improve separately, and what kinds not to waste time on. They even signal when continuous improvement is more likely to create competitive disadvantage rather than competitive advantage.

## UCA Initiatives Should Take Priority

Understanding what work falls under which categories requires a clear understanding of the company's strategy. The initiatives resulting from an audit that affect the Unit of Competitive Advantage work processes should clearly have the highest priority among improvement projects. Value-added support initiatives should be second priority, and essential support work should be the third priority. Nonessential work should not be continued.

Once improvement opportunities that will have the greatest impact on the achievement of the company's goals have been identified, the following ideas can be used to lend further insight into how opportunities identified through an audit should be prioritized:

- *Focus on the two or three most important areas.*

Insisting that action be taken on all of the problems uncovered by the audit may overwhelm the people who are responsible for bringing about those changes. Flatter organizations and leaner work forces mean that people are already being asked to do more work with fewer resources and less time. Producing a long list of improvement initiatives may prompt people to dismiss all of them because they don't have time to complete the whole list.

- *Focus on the areas that can be changed.*

Emphasizing problems that are beyond the control of the people who are responsible to work on process improvement only leads to cynicism and a sense of powerlessness. By focusing on things that are within the sphere of influence, accountability for each part of the action plan can be clearly defined.

- *Include as priorities some improvements that can be made quickly.*

Rapid, visible improvement helps build support for more complicated initiatives. Quick improvements also reassure people of management's support for long-term improvement. Seeing immediate improvement helps to build commitment at all levels to the process, and helps build momentum for further change.

- *Emphasize the improvements that seem essential to long-term success.*

Essential improvements may involve sensitive issues or difficult problems, such as deficiencies in fundamental skill levels within the organization or basic strategy issues. These problems are not only difficult and expensive to address, but may also cause a great deal of personal pain or require significant individual adjustment. Nevertheless, long-term improvement requires a commitment to dealing with difficult issues rather than avoiding them.

# Sharing Audit Results

In most cases, audit results will be presented to various interested people in a feedback meeting. Those in attendance may include members of the executive team, managers who work in the area covered by the audit, the audit team members, and anyone else who is affected by or interested in the results. The meeting should be conducted by members of the audit team. The purpose is to present their findings, and make recommendations for capitalizing on opportunities for improvement.

## Conducting Effective Feedback Meetings

The audit team's strategy for the meeting should be to present a clear and simple picture of the current situation as revealed by the audit. This may be a moment of truth for those who have been anticipating the audit results. The feedback meeting for an audit holds both excitement and anxiety: excitement that the future will be bright, and anxiety that shortcomings in individual performance will be highlighted and demands made for personal change. As a result, the meeting must be carefully managed in order to lead to productive change. The following structure is one recommended format for conducting a feedback meeting.

- *Introduce the meeting and preview its agenda.*

This might include an overview of the original intent of the audit, introduction of the audit team, and a brief summary of the meeting's agenda. This step should take no more than five minutes.

- *Present the audit findings.*

Audit findings should summarize the most important points revealed by the data gathered in the audit process. They should be presented separately from the audit recommendations in order to allow people to digest the two parts of the presentation separately. Clearing up misunderstandings about the findings may make the group more accepting of the team's recommendations.

The presentation of the audit findings should take comparatively little time. Audits almost always generate much more data than can be effectively presented or digested in a feedback meeting. The goal of the audit team should be to zero in on the two or three most important points learned from the audit, and present enough supporting data to illustrate those points.

# THE STRATEGIC MARKETING PLAN AUDIT

Presenting too much data about audit findings has a number of negative effects. It encourages people to conduct their own analysis of the audit data. To a certain extent, this is a healthy and normal reaction. If others understand the evidence that supports the conclusions drawn by the audit team, they are more likely to accept and own the audit results. Therefore, they will be more committed to the changes brought about by the audit results. However, when people immerse themselves in large amounts of data, they may become victims of "analysis paralysis": they may spend unnecessary time attempting to explain contradictory data, or trying to understand methods used by others to gather data.

- *Present audit recommendations.*

Presenting the audit recommendations should be the central point of the meeting. The recommendations should grow out of the data highlights presented. The audit team should view the recommendations as discussion points for the meeting, rather than as absolute action items.

A common mistake in feedback meetings is to spend most of the meeting on presenting data and recommendations. It is easy for audit team members to become enamored of data they have invested considerable time and energy to collect and analyze. Others in the audience will probably also be interested in the details of the data collected. However, if too much time is spent on discussing the recommendations, the meeting will end before a commitment to action has been made.

- *Ask others to react to the data.*

The reactions of top management and those responsible for implementing audit recommendations will determine the ultimate value of the audit data. Therefore, the feedback meeting is a good time to resolve questions or problems with the findings and recommendations as they have been presented. If resistance to the audit findings is not resolved in the feedback meeting, opportunities for improvement may be lost.

Those attending the meeting may offer their opinions willingly. If not, the audit team members should ask the others in the room for their reaction to what has been presented.

- *Develop preliminary action plans.*

The detailed action plans should grow out of the recommendations made by the audit team. They should specifically address the question of who should do what by when. Formal accountability mechanisms should be established before the end of the meeting, such as the scheduling of subsequent meetings or follow-up check points.

# WRITING EFFECTIVE AUDIT REPORTS

There are three fundamental purposes for writing a formal report at the conclusion of an audit:

- An audit report may be a stand-alone summary of the audit. This approach is not recommended, inasmuch as the report is likely to be filed away, making the probability of action unlikely.

- The report may supplement a feedback meeting, providing those in attendance with documentation and an outline to follow.

- The report should also serve as a baseline document to make measurement of performance improvement possible in future audits.

Because the written report is the most enduring part of the audit presentation, it should be well written and easy to understand. The following tips will lead to the preparation of effective written audit reports.

**Focus on a Few Key Points**

The audit presentation should focus on the two or three most important findings. It is impossible to present all of the data gathered in the audit to those who were not on the audit team. It is also not advisable to present every detail of the data. The audit team members should trust their own judgment about what the highlights of the study were, and present enough data to support that judgment. For each of the major findings, the team may want to include the following information:

- What is the problem?

- Why does it exist?

- What happens if the problem is not fixed:

    — in the short term?

    — in the long term?

- Recommend solutions.

- Outline expected benefits.

# THE STRATEGIC MARKETING PLAN AUDIT

**Prepare an Outline Before Writing the First Draft**

A good outline ensures that the logic of the report is clear, and that ideas proceed in an order that makes sense. The following outline provides one approach that works effectively.

*Background*

This section should establish the framework for the audit in terms of:

- Providing a brief discussion of the overall purpose of the audit.

- Identifying the role of the audit team in the overall process.

- Establishing the limitations of the audit methodology to ensure that others utilize the results provided in the report appropriately.

*Objectives*

This section should identify specific objectives of the audit in terms of types of information the team was expected to generate.

*Methodology*

The methodology section should describe the mechanics of the audit and include the following information:

- Types of assessment used (survey, interviews, focus groups, etc.).

- Data sources, or the sample groups for each of the types of assessment used.

- Time frame during which the audit was conducted.

- Other pertinent details about how the audit was conducted.

*Findings*

This section is designed to provide others with a review of the "facts" that came out of the audit. Except in cases where an audit checks regulatory compliance, only the most significant findings should be discussed in any detail in the report. This section should also include briefly presented data supporting the findings.

# THE STRATEGIC MARKETING PLAN AUDIT

*Conclusions*

This section should report the audit team's interpretation of what the facts of the audit mean in light of the objectives stated at the outset of the audit.

*Recommendations*

This section includes suggestions from the audit team on how to close the performance gaps identified in the audit. The degree of specificity to be included in the audit report will vary from company to company and audit to audit.

*Appendix*

This portion of the formal report should include any of the following items that are relevant to the audit:

- A copy of any questionnaires or survey instruments used in the audit.

- A summary of the data gathered in the course of the audit.

- Recommendations for subsequent audits based on the team's experience.

## Present Audit Findings Accurately

Those who read the report will no doubt be somewhat familiar with the area covered by the audit. They may notice discrepancies between what they know about the subject and what is reported in the written document. Spotting one inaccuracy may lead the readers to discredit all of the findings, conclusions and recommendations. Audit team members should be careful to report data as it was actually generated, and to describe the impact of the findings accurately.

## Use Clear, Concise Language

Every statement included in the report should be based on sound evidence developed or reviewed during the audit. Whatever is said must be supported or supportable. Speculation should be avoided. Generalities and vague reporting will only confuse and mislead those that the report should influence or inform. For example, a report using the terms some, a few, or not all can leave the reader confused about the significance of the finding. Specific quantities should be used, such as, "of the ten samples taken, two were found to be...", "Three of five respondents said that...", and so on. Statements should be qualified as needed, and any unconfirmed data or information should be identified as such.

Ideas or sentences that do not amplify the central theme should be eliminated. The report should not identify individuals or highlight the mistakes of individuals.

**Use Good Grammar and Style**

Basic grammar and style rules should be followed in writing the text. Below are some examples:

- Avoid extreme terms, such as alarming, deplorable, gross negligence, etc.

- Avoid using redundant or lengthy phrases, such as calling something an emergency situation when the word emergency alone will do.

- Avoid verbs camouflaged as nouns or adjectives. For example, use "the new procedure will reduce error entries," rather than "The new procedure will accomplish a reduction of error entries."

- Avoid indirect expressions where possible. For example, "Many instances of poor management were found," is more direct than saying, "There were many instances of poor judgment found."

- Use short, familiar words. Use words that are easily understandable to everyone and that convey the message concisely.

- Keep sentences short. Most writing experts suggest that an average sentence should be between 15 and 18 words. Packing too many ideas into a single sentence confuses and tires readers.

The audit team should provide enough background information in the report so that the reader clearly understands who conducted the audit and what the audit did or did not include. The purpose of the report as well as the purpose and scope of the audit should also be described in a manner that enables the reader to know why the report was written and who should take corrective action.

**Timing of the Report**

The timing of audit reports is critical to the overall reporting process and must be carefully thought out. In many cases, a written draft of the audit report is prepared one to three weeks before the feedback meeting. This draft then goes through a review and another report is prepared in time for the team's presentation. A final report may be completed after the feedback session has been held in order to record changes resulting from that meeting.

THE STRATEGIC MARKETING PLAN AUDIT

# DEALING WITH RESISTANCE TO RECOMMENDATIONS

Most audit teams feel that if they can present their ideas clearly and logically, and have the best interests of the company or department at heart, managers will accept the recommendations made as part of the audit and follow the team's recommendations. Many people who have worked in organizations, however, find that no matter how reasonably recommendations are presented, they are all too often not implemented.

Implementation usually fails because it requires people to change their ways of working. That change requires a great deal of effort, energy, and risk; therefore, change is usually resisted. Resistance is an emotional process; people may embrace recommendations based on their logic, but fail to implement them because of the emotional resistance to the personal change involved. Resistance is a predictable, natural, and necessary part of the learning process. Although resistance may cause audit team members to feel they have missed the mark in terms of the recommendations they have made, it actually often signals accuracy in having interpreted the organization's needs. By dealing with the resistance directly, audit teams can work through barriers to implementing process improvements.

**What Are the Signs of Resistance?**

In many cases, resistance may be expressed directly. Direct objections to recommendations are relatively easy to address, inasmuch as they can be discussed and resolved. When recommendations are being presented, team members should stop frequently to allow those who are listening to the report to voice any objections or disagreements. Those who are presenting the data should be careful not to become defensive or to punish those who express reservations about the recommendations. It is impossible to deal with objections unless they are voiced; therefore, the audit team should welcome the expression of objections or differences of opinion. The following tips may be used for surfacing and dealing with direct resistance:

- Provide many opportunities for others to express their concerns.

- Carefully clarify any confusing concerns.

- Deal with important or easy concerns immediately. Defer the remainder.

- Summarize the concerns before moving on. Show that concerns have been heard.

- It may even be helpful to list concerns on a flip chart or blackboard.

If direct resistance continues, the following steps may be necessary:

- Talk about the differences of opinion.

- Voice concern and support for negotiating a resolution.

- Avoid struggles for control of the situation.

**Dealing with Indirect Resistance**

In other cases, resistance may be subtle and elusive. Indirect resistance is difficult to identify and deal with because its manifestations seem logical. People who are experiencing indirect resistance may feel that they are "getting the run around." Many different forms of resistance may manifest themselves in a single meeting:

- Request for more detail.

- Providing too much detail in response to questions.

- Complaining that there isn't enough time to implement recommendations.

- Claiming that the recommendations are impractical.

- Attacking those who propose improvement initiatives.

- Acting confused.

- Responding with silence.

- Intellectualizing about the data.

- Moralizing that problems wouldn't exist if it weren't for "those people".

- Agreeing to implement recommendations with no intention of acting on them.

- Asking questions about methodology.

- Arguing that previous problems have resolved themselves.

- Focusing on solutions before findings are fully understood.

Almost any of these responses is legitimate in moderate amounts. For example, members of the group may have concerns about the audit's methodology that should be considered. Managers may realistically wonder where they will find the time to implement recommendations. However, if refusal to act on recommendations persists once legitimate concerns have been addressed, then the audit team is probably facing indirect resistance.

Many models used in sales training provide recommendations for overcoming resistance. These methods suggest the use of data and logical arguments to win the point and convince the other person to buy whatever is being sold. These models work well for direct resistance. However, indirect resistance is normally based on feelings rather than logic. Therefore, the only way to truly overcome resistance is to deal with the emotional processes that cause it to happen in the first place. It is almost impossible to talk people out of the way they feel.

Feelings pass and change when they are expressed directly. A key skill for audit teams that are attempting to implement recommendations is to ask the people who are presenting resistance to put directly into words what they are experiencing. The most effective way to make this happen is for the audit team members to address directly what is happening in the situation. The following keys provide help in surfacing and dealing with indirect resistance.

- *Work once or twice with the person's concern, even when it feels as if he or she is resisting recommendations.*

By attempting to work with the problem stated by the person raising a concern, audit team members can determine whether the concern is legitimate or whether it is an excuse for not taking action. If the issues raised are legitimate, the person should show some willingness to discuss and resolve them. If the issues are manifestations of indirect resistance, the person will probably respond with other forms of resistance.

- *Identify the form the resistance is taking.*

Paying attention to the dynamics of a discussion can provide important clues as to whether or not a person is resisting recommendations. If a person is consistently distancing him or herself from those who are presenting the audit findings, using gestures or postures that suggest tension or discomfort, while at the same time presenting arguments for why the recommendations presented are inappropriate, it is probably a sign of resistance. The non-verbal responses of the presenters may also signal the onset of resistance. If presenters feel that they are suppressing negative feelings or becoming bored or irritated, it may be further evidence that the client is resisting.

Once presenters become aware of the resistance, the next step is to put it into words. This is best done by using neutral, everyday language. The skill is to describe the form of the resistance in a way that encourages the person to make a more direct statement of the reservation he or she is experiencing.

One general rule for stating what type of resistance is being manifested is to phrase the statement in common, non-threatening language. Statements should be made in the same tone and language that would be used to address a problem with a spouse or close friend. The statement should be made with as little evaluation as possible; it is the presenter's observation about what is happening in the situation.

A second general rule for surfacing indirect resistance involves not talking for a couple of moments after the presenter has stated what he or she has observed. There may be a temptation to elaborate on the observation, or to support it with evidence. However, continuing the statement will reduce the tension in the situation. Without tension, the person who is resisting feels no discomfort, and is unlikely to address the issue directly. Moreover, elaborating on the original statement may increase the other person's defensiveness and reduce the chances of solving the problem.

If stating the problem in direct, non-punishing terms fails to bring the resistance out into the open, there may be little more the audit team can do to overcome the indirect resistance. The best strategy in this case is to avoid resisting the resistance. Team members should support the person who is resisting and proceed with the implementation of recommendations to the extent possible.

THE STRATEGIC MARKETING PLAN AUDIT

# BUILDING AN ONGOING AUDIT PROGRAM

As the pace of change increases, and as organization leaders become more and more committed to continuously improving their effectiveness and efficiency, audits of all types of processes will become more common. The most effective companies will establish program of ongoing audits, whereby a number of goals can be accomplished:

- Performance improvements can be measured over time.

- Important changes in the company's environment can be systematically monitored.

- Managers can make a habit of change and improvement, rather than resisting it.

- Those areas that are of highest importance to the company can be routinely improved.

- Processes can be modified to be in alignment with changes in strategy or in the environment.

As with all management techniques, however, an enduring program of ongoing audits requires that audits become integrated into the overall management system. The following guidelines are keys to weaving audits into the fabric of day-to-day operations.

**Establish Support for Ongoing Audits**

While support for audits begins at the executive level, ownership for the audit process must be felt throughout the organization if an ongoing program is to be successful. The following actions will help to broaden support for the audit process, while ensuring greater benefit from the audit.

- *Share the results of the audit with everyone throughout the organization.*

By keeping others informed about the results of an audit, managers reassure those who participate in and are affected by the audit of the integrity of the process. Employees sometimes become suspicious of probing investigators; they may have doubts about how the information will be used, or whether the information will be used. By sharing audit results, managers make an implicit commitment to improving the processes that have been evaluated.

- *Act on the audit results.*

Questions will be raised about continuing audits if early assessments bear no fruits. Failing to act on performance gaps that are identified leads to cynicism and lack of trust among those who work with the problems daily. On the other hand, improving a process can create the momentum that comes from accomplishment. Committing resources and attention to the improvement opportunities revealed by an audit also shows management commitment to the improvement process.

- *Let others know when performance has improved.*

Communicating the positive results from an audit is one way of rewarding the people who contributed to that improvement. It also builds faith in the effectiveness of the audit process. Moreover, showing that performance has improved is another means of reassuring people of a commitment to the improvement process.

- *Reward people for their part in improvements.*

Increasing efficiency and effectiveness can often be a threatening experience for those who are involved in a work process. Improving the way resources are used often means eliminating the need for some of the people who have been involved in the process. Although flatter, leaner organizations often preclude the possibility of offering promotions, managers should nevertheless attempt to ensure that people who contribute to performance improvement find their own situations better rather than worse as a result.

Rewards for helping to close performance gaps may span a range from thanking people for their efforts to planning a group celebration to offering bonuses or pay increases for improvement. Rewards are especially meaningful when people are allowed to suggest what rewards they would like for their contribution. This may provide managers with new ideas for rewards that may be less costly to the organization than financial recognition.

- *Involve a wide variety of people in the audit process.*

People can be involved in the audit process in many ways. By involving people from a broad spectrum, more people learn about audit techniques and results, thus spreading commitment to the audit process throughout the organization. By involving many people in the data-gathering process, employees feel that action plans growing out of the audit were a result of their input. Excluding people from the data-gathering phase usually reduces the feeling of ownership for the results, thus making people feel as if initiatives are being imposed on them. By the same token, involving a broad range of people in the development of action plans expands ownership for the plans and allows for the generation of more ideas.

*Part* 3

# IMPLEMENTING A STRATEGIC MARKETING PLAN AUDIT: QUESTIONS AND CHECKLISTS

This section of the Strategic Marketing Plan Audit comprises a series of questions based on the ten steps given in Part 1. These questions have been designed to help you plan and implement your audit in a straightforward and practical manner, covering all the relevant parts of the audit in the correct sequence.

**Ten steps to auditing a company's strategic marketing plan**

- Step 1 Executive Summary
- Step 2 Background
- Step 3 Mission Statement
- Step 4 Marketing Appreciation
- Step 5 Conclusions and Key Assumptions
- Step 6 Strategic Objectives
- Step 7 Core Strategy
- Step 8 Key Policies
- Step 9 Administration and Control
- Step 10 Communication and Timing

*Note*: Before you look at the questions, do read the audit introduction along with the overview *The Nature of Strategic Marketing Planning*. Additionally, useful background information is given for each step before the questions are listed.

*Step* **1**

# EXECUTIVE SUMMARY

### BACKGROUND INFORMATION

Although this should appear first in the strategic marketing plan, it should be written as the last stage. It needs to be a clear and concise summary of the key issues in the plan and should help guide more detailed analysis.

To avoid the executive summary being too long or too short, extensive cross-referencing is advised. Hence any point and argument can be looked at for further detail in the main body of the report.

In the "Questions" section below you will find a set of questions that will provide an overview of what an executive summary of a strategic marketing plan should cover.

### QUESTIONS

- Given that the executive summary needs to be a synopsis of the whole strategic marketing plan, is it:
  - ❏ clear
  - ❏ logical
  - ❏ well structured
  - ❏ informative
  - ❏ easy to read?

- Does it capture the reader's attention and make it precisely clear what benefits will be gained by reading it?

- Does it also generate enthusiasm and conviction?

- Whether you are part of a large multidivisional organization or a small company, are you aware that the executive summary is your one chance to make a good first impression?

- Does your executive summary make clear:
  - ❏ what the plan is about and what the objectives are
  - ❏ who is involved (e.g. customers, key suppliers, competitors)

- ❏ why you should be preferred (i.e. what is the source of your competitive advantage)
- ❏ where you will compete
- ❏ how you will compete
- ❏ when (i.e. what the critical timings are)?

• In order to convert opinion and judgment into numerical measures, have you constructed a factor rating table?

*Note*: Three pieces of information are required to construct a factor rating table. These are:

1. What are the critical/relevant factors?

2. What weighting do you assign to each of these?

3. How do you and your competitors score on these factors?

An example of a rating table across five important dimensions – price, performance, reliability, service and delivery – is provided in Table 2, Step 1 of Part 1.

*Having completed the questions in Step 1 and understood the factors to be taken into consideration when auditing an executive summary, the next step covers the background statement. Extensive information for this is given in Step 2 of Part 1. A list of appropriate audit questions follows an outline of this step.*

## Step 2

# BACKGROUND

**BACKGROUND INFORMATION**

The background statement is another important component of the strategic marketing plan. It positions the whole plan in the reader's mind and provides a common point of departure.

Rarely is there a shared common understanding and purpose within an organization. The norm is more likely to be that everyone within that organization has their own view on the current position. At the same time, those outside the organization have diverse perceptions of it. So it is essential to develop a clear statement of the organization's current position in order to determine future courses of action.

In the "Questions" section below you will find a set of questions that will assist in understanding and formulating a good background statement.

**QUESTIONS**

- Does your background statement cover the following key aspects:
  - ❏ name of the organization
  - ❏ when it was established
  - ❏ what it does (products or services)
  - ❏ who its customers are
  - ❏ how big it is
  - ❏ stage of industry lifecycle
  - ❏ who and what are its major competitors
  - ❏ what the major issues facing the organization are (e.g. political, economic, technological)?

- Did you know that good examples of the information required in a background statement are to be found in the information stockbrokers circulate to their clients as the basis for deciding whether or not to invest in a company?

*Note*: Examples of this type of stockbroker information (in this case SBC Warburg Dillon Read Small Companies Quarterly Report) is provided in Step 2 of Part 1.

*Having written the background statement and included all the necessary components, the next part of the strategic marketing plan to come under scrutiny is the mission statement. Guidelines for this are found in Step 3 of Part 1. A brief list of appropriate audit questions follows an outline of this step.*

# Step 3

# MISSION STATEMENT

### BACKGROUND INFORMATION

In recent years corporate management has come to see the importance of corporate culture and value, and of having a formal mission statement. Capturing and communicating the nature of the company's mission is seen as the 'glue' that holds the organization together.

In small companies the mission may be implicit but clearly understood, whereas in larger organizations it may be explicit, written down and widely communicated, but still not understood as well.

The mission reflects cultural norms and values and is the organization's reason for being. By contrast, the vision represents the current leader's interpretation of the achievement of the mission. Meanwhile, strategy is the means by which specific action plans are measured against the benchmark of the vision.

In the "Questions" section below you will find a set of questions that will clarify what a mission statement is and will assist in writing your own.

### QUESTIONS

- Are you aware of the following terms (from *Long Range Planning*, Klemm et al) that embrace the concept of a formal declaration:
  - ❏ mission statement
  - ❏ corporate statement
  - ❏ aims and values
  - ❏ purpose
  - ❏ principles
  - ❏ objectives
  - ❏ goals
  - ❏ responsibilities and obligations?

- Are you also aware of the following hierarchy in the use of these terms (Klemm et al):
  - ❏ Statement 1: The Mission (statement of the long-term purpose of the organization reflecting deeply held corporate views)

# The Strategic Marketing Plan Audit

❑ Statement 2: Strategic Objectives (statement of long-term strategic objectives outlining desired direction and performance in broad terms)

❑ Statement 3: Quantified Planning Targets (objectives in the form of quantified planning targets over a specific period)

❑ Statement 4: The Business Definition (statement outlining the scope and activities of the company)?

- Given that the mission is highly specific to your organization, is it being articulated by those currently responsible for its culture and values?

- Does your organization already have a formal, written mission statement which can be used in this section of the strategic marketing plan?

- If the mission statement has to be written, will you ensure that the endorsement of both management and employees is secured?

*Having thought through a mission statement that covers the organization's character, identity and reasons for existence, why the organization exists and for whose benefits, the beliefs and moral principles driving the organization's behavior, and its norms and rules of conduct, the next step involves market appreciation. Extensive information for this is given in Step 4 of Part 1. A list of appropriate audit questions follows an outline of this step.*

## Step 4

# MARKETING APPRECIATION

**BACKGROUND INFORMATION**

A market appreciation analysis involves the following three elements.

1. Macroenvironmental Analysis.

2. Microenvironmental Analysis.

3. Self-Analysis.

These three elements are then combined into a SWOT analysis which summarizes the strengths and weaknesses of the organization in relation to the opportunities and threats that it faces.

In the "Questions" section below are a series of questions that will take you through these three elements and assist in the preparation of a SWOT analysis.

**QUESTIONS**

*1. Macroenvironmental Analysis*

- Given that a macroenvironmental analysis looks to provide information about events and relationships in an organization's future environment, are you aware that environmental analysis is responsible for these three main activities:

  ❏ generation of an up-to-date database of information on the changing business scene

  ❏ alerting management to what is happening in the marketplace and the industry

  ❏ disseminating important information and analyses to key strategic decision makers within the organization?

- In establishing a formal environmental analysis function, have all the following key criteria been satisfied:

  ❏ environmental trends, events and issues must be reviewed on a regular basis

  ❏ criteria have been established against which the monitored trends can be evaluated

  ❏ the monitoring of trends should be guided by written procedures

  ❏ responsibility for the implementation of these written procedures must be clearly assigned?

- If environmental analysis is already embedded in a corporate strategy-making unit, is it expected to provide a broad view of possible future changes in the business environment?

- Is it expected that environmental analysis should arm the company's strategic decision makers with information, analyses and forecasts relevant to the strategies governing how the company is to respond to the changing business environment?

- Does it also provide a basis for questioning the assumptions underpinning the company's strategic thinking and for generating new assumptions?

2. *Microenvironmental Analysis*

- Given that microenvironmental analysis is concerned with the specific factors influencing the company's competitive strategy, is yours comprised of:
    - ❏ industry/market analysis
    - ❏ competitor analysis
    - ❏ customer analysis?

- Have you used value chain analysis to evaluate your company's industry and the markets in which it operates?

*Note*: Value chain analysis was developed by McKinsey & Co in the 1960s as a tool for evaluating competition. Figure 3, Step 4 of Part 1 shows the six basis elements or subsystems of the analysis – raw materials, production, wholesale distribution, retail distribution, consumer or user, and after-sales service.

- Have you examined each of the subsystems of the value chain analysis to establish the interrelationship and interdependence between them in terms of:
    - ❏ the degree of competition within and between each subsystem (and hence the number of competitors, their profitability, their degree of integration, their cost structure and the existence and nature of any barriers to entry)
    - ❏ where, in the total system, value is added by the activities of the production, distribution, or servicing subsystems
    - ❏ the location of economic leverage within the system
    - ❏ the location of marketing leverage within the system?

- Having completed the value chain analysis, have you gone on to identify companies in direct competition with you?

# The Strategic Marketing Plan Audit

- Once you have identified the relevant competitors, have they been evaluated in terms of the critical success factors determining performance in your industry?

- Does your competitor analysis include:
  - ❏ details of their products or services
  - ❏ explanation of what benefits their products or services offer
  - ❏ analysis of how they compare in appearance, price and performance
  - ❏ whether they have any significant strength or advantage over you
  - ❏ whether they have any significant weaknesses that could be exploited
  - ❏ whether they are growing, stable, or declining?

*Note*: Table 3, Step 4 of Part 1 gives an example of some of the questions you might want to use to identify competitive substitutes.

- Having identified the relevant competitors, have you then evaluated them in terms of the critical success factors determining performance in your industry?

- As the last part of the microenvironmental analysis, have you conducted a customer analysis?

- In performing your customer analysis, were you aware that the seller must define carefully both the objective needs customers are seeking to satisfy as well as the subjective factors influencing or modifying the individual's perception of the objective factors?

*Note*: Table 4, Step 4 of Part 1 provides a listing of the sort of factors to be evaluated when undertaking a customer analysis.

## 3. Self-Analysis

- Were you aware of the need to conduct an internal audit as part of the marketing appreciation in order to identify and evaluate assets, resources, skills and competencies?

- Were you aware that the internal audit should include all of the following resources:
  - ❏ physical (i.e. land, buildings, availability of and access to utilities and transportation, plant and equipment)
  - ❏ technical
  - ❏ financial

# The Strategic Marketing Plan Audit

- ❏ purchasing
- ❏ labor
- ❏ marketing?

- Were you also aware that the value of an internal audit is only ascertained by comparison with similar data for competing companies?

- When complete, does your internal appraisal provide answers to all the following questions:
  - ❏ What is the company's present position?
  - ❏ What is the company good at?
  - ❏ What are the main problems faced?
  - ❏ What is the company poor at?
  - ❏ What major resources and expertise exist?
  - ❏ What major resources and expertise deficiencies exist?

*SWOT Analysis*

- Does the summary statement of the SWOT analysis contain all the key findings from the market appreciation?

- Are all the findings correctly classified (i.e. strengths can be weaknesses and vice versa)?

*Having written the marketing appreciation covering the macro environment, the micro environment, an internal audit, and a SWOT analysis, the next stage of the strategic marketing plan audit concerns the conclusions and key assumptions. This is covered in detail in Step 5 of Part 1. A brief list of appropriate audit questions follows an outline of this step.*

## Step 5

# CONCLUSIONS AND KEY ASSUMPTIONS

### BACKGROUND INFORMATION

This part of the strategic marketing plan provides a link between the following two questions.

- Where are we now?
- Where do we want to go?

The answers to the first question should come from the SWOT analysis and the other analyses. To establish future objectives and formulate a strategy, you will need to make certain assumptions about your conclusions and how they could change in the future.

In analyzing the data, three different levels are apparent.

1. Deduction.
2. Inference.
3. Formulation of assumptions.

In the "Questions" section below is a set of questions aimed at distinguishing these three levels of data analysis.

### QUESTIONS

*1. Deduction*

- Did you know that a deduction is defined as making a logically necessary conclusion about a specific case from perfect information concerning the general case?

*2. Inference*

- Did you know that an inference is defined as the interpretation placed on evidence by an observer?

- Therefore were you also aware that an inference can range from excellent to very poor?

# THE STRATEGIC MARKETING PLAN AUDIT

*3. Formulation of assumptions*

- Given that the need for assumptions only arises when there is an absence of evidence necessary to link other information having a bearing on the problem, were you aware of the two kinds of assumptions:

    ❏ working assumptions

    ❏ critical assumptions?

- Having compiled the conclusions, are they clear, logical and derived from the marketing appreciation?

- Do the assumptions cover the critical issues where you lack objective data?

- Are the assumptions clearly stated and justified by reference to known facts?

*Having written the conclusions and key assumptions covering both where the organization is now and where it wants to go, the audit team should now turn its attention to strategic objectives. Details for this are provided in Step 6 of Part 1. A brief list of appropriate audit questions follows an outline of this step.*

# STRATEGIC OBJECTIVES

**BACKGROUND INFORMATION**

A key part of any management role is determining a course of action which will realize the maximum potential of all their resources including labor, physical, financial and technological. This involves identifying the various possibilities and then selecting a strategy. However, alongside any strategic planning must run a system for monitoring achievement.

In this section we will look at three basic strategic marketing objectives.

1. To enlarge the market.

2. To increase market share.

3. To improve profitability.

*Note*: These three basic marketing objectives are taken from McKay's *Marketing Mystique*.

In the "Questions" section below you will find a set of questions to assist in formulating a variety of strategies that will achieve these three objectives.

**QUESTIONS**

- Do your strategic objectives satisfy at least the following three objectives:
  - ❏ they must define a precise end result
  - ❏ they must set out the conditions and assumptions on which they are based
  - ❏ they must spell out the performance indicators and timetable to be used in assessing their achievement?

*1. To enlarge the market*

- If one of your strategic marketing objectives is to enlarge the market, will it be achieved:
  - ❏ by innovation or product development
  - ❏ by innovation or market development?

# The Strategic Marketing Plan Audit

- If you aim to achieve it by innovation or product development, will it be:
  - ❏ through improving existing products or lines to increase use
  - ❏ through developing new products or lines?

- If you aim to achieve it by innovation or market development, will it be:
  - ❏ through developing present end-use markets
  - ❏ through discovering new end-use markets?

2. *To increase market share*

- If another of your strategic objectives is to increase market share for competitive advantage, will it be achieved:
  - ❏ by emphasizing product development and product improvement
  - ❏ by emphasizing persuasion effort
  - ❏ by emphasizing customer-service activities?

- If you aim to emphasize product development and product improvement, will it be:
  - ❏ through product performance
  - ❏ through product quality
  - ❏ through product features?

- If you aim to emphasize persuasion effort, will it be:
  - ❏ through sales and distribution
  - ❏ through advertising and sales promotion?

- If you aim to emphasize customer-service activities, will it be:
  - ❏ through ready availability, order handling and delivery service
  - ❏ through credit and collection policies
  - ❏ through after-sales product service?

3. *To improve profitability*

To improve profitability, will you choose to emphasize:
- sales volume for profit leverage
- elimination of unprofitable activities
- price improvement
- cost reduction?

# THE STRATEGIC MARKETING PLAN AUDIT

- If you aim to improve profitability by emphasizing sales volume for profit leverage, will it be:

  ❏ through strengthened sales and distribution effort

  ❏ through strengthened advertising and sales promotion effort

  ❏ through strengthened advertising effort?

- If you aim to improve profitability by emphasizing elimination of unprofitable activities, will it be:

  ❏ through pruning products and services

  ❏ through pruning sales coverage and distribution

  ❏ through pruning customer services?

- If you aim to improve profitability by emphasizing price improvement, will it be:

  ❏ through leadership in initiating needed price increases

  ❏ through differentiating products and service from those of your competitors?

- Finally, if you aim to improve profitability by emphasizing cost reduction, will it be through improved effectiveness of marketing tools and methods in product planning, in persuasion activities and in customer service activities?

*Having written up the strategic objectives, the audit team now needs to look at the core strategy. Details for this are given in Step 7 of Part 1. A brief list of appropriate audit questions follows an outline of this step.*

## Step 7

# CORE STRATEGY

### BACKGROUND INFORMATION

The core strategy of the marketing plan can be viewed as one of three choices:

- undifferentiated
- differentiated, and
- concentrated.

Having made your choice, writing your core strategy statement should include justification of why the particular strategy has been selected.

In the "Questions" section below you will find a set a questions to take you through the preparation for writing up your core strategy statement.

### QUESTIONS

- Is your strategy:
  - ❏ undifferentiated
  - ❏ differentiated
  - ❏ concentrated (focus)?

*Note*: Table 5, Step 7 of Part 1 provides a list of the key characteristics of these three strategies.

- Does your plan have a clear statement of the core strategy to be followed?

- Is the core strategy supported by a short statement justifying its selection?

*Note*: Table 6, Step 7 of Part 1 lists some of the key questions to ask yourself when selecting a core strategy.

- If your company is large, will you go for the usual undifferentiated strategy where you have a unique product with mass market appeal enabling you to maintain your scale economies and market leadership?

- If your company is large and the market is segmented, will you go for a differentiated strategy and develop specific products for all market segments?

# THE STRATEGIC MARKETING PLAN AUDIT

- If your company is medium-sized and caters for two or more segments, will you also go for a differentiated strategy?

- If your company is small and only caters for one segment, will you pursue a focus strategy?

*Having completed the core strategy statement, the audit team should move on to Step 8 which covers key policies. Information for this is given in Step 8 of Part 1. A brief list of appropriate audit questions follows an outline of this step.*

# KEY POLICIES

**BACKGROUND INFORMATION**

Having set the objectives, you must next address how you're actually going to achieve them and this requires the development of a marketing mix or program. This marketing mix will vary from industry to industry, from company to company, and quite often during the life of the product or service itself.

In tailoring its mix, a company will want to offer the one that target customers will see as superior to those offered by its competitors (known as the differential advantage).

For the purposes of this audit, the marketing mix will be viewed in terms of the 4Ps: product, price, promotion and place.

*Note*: The 4Ps are elaborated in Table 7, Step 8 of Part 1.

In the "Questions" section below you will find a set of key questions for the 4Ps that need to be addressed.

**QUESTIONS**

*Product Policy*

- Have all the following questions regarding the product been addressed?
    - ❏ At what stage in its lifecycle is the product – introduction/growth/maturity/decline?
    - ❏ Is demand elastic or inelastic?
    - ❏ Is the product differentiated or undifferentiated?
    - ❏ Is the product pushed into the market via distributors or pulled using advertising and promotion?
    - ❏ Are sales growing/stable/declining?
    - ❏ Are there close substitutes for the product?
    - ❏ How well does the product meet user needs – excellent/good/fair/poor?
    - ❏ What proportion of sales are attributable to products launched in the last five years?
    - ❏ What plans are there for new product development?

*Price Policy*

- Have all the following questions regarding price been addressed?
  - Is there a clear statement of factors influencing pricing decisions?
  - Is there a clear pricing objective and if so what is it?
  - Is explicit account taken of cost, demand and competition in developing the policy?
  - What strategy – skimming (high) or penetration (low) – are you following, and why?
  - How important is price in the marketing mix as a whole?
  - Is there a clear statement and justification of the method chosen?

*Distribution Policy*

- Have all the following questions regarding distribution been addressed?
  - Is distribution exclusive, selective or intensive, and why?
  - How long are channels of distribution?
  - How many and what kinds of intermediary are involved?
  - Who controls the channel?

*Promotion Policy*

- Have all the following questions regarding promotion been addressed?
  - What is the promotional objective?
  - How will achievement of this objective be measured?
  - What do you want to tell the target audience?
  - How do you intend to tell them?
  - What vehicle or medium do you intend to use, and in what proportions?
  - What is the balance between personal (selling) and impersonal (advertising, sales promotion) methods?
  - What measures are to be used to measure the effectiveness of the chosen methods?

- Having assessed these four individual policies, have you checked whether they are consistent with each other?

- Are they also adequately integrated into a coherent whole?

*Having completed the preparation for writing up key policies, the audit team will now need to turn to administration and control. This is covered in Step 9 of Part 1. A brief list of appropriate audit questions follows an outline of this step.*

# Administration and Control

### BACKGROUND INFORMATION

This section of the strategic marketing plan concentrates on allocating responsibility for proposal implementation, stating areas of responsibility and authority, dealing with lines of reporting and control, outlining measures to monitor performance, and giving a complete budget for the marketing function.

It is also the point at which the audit team can assess the overall validity of the strategic marketing plan.

In the "Questions" section below you will find a set of questions that will help you to assess this section of the marketing plan.

### QUESTIONS

- Does the administration and control section of your strategic marketing plan fulfill all of the following:
  ❏ sets out who is to be responsible for implementing the proposals it contains
  ❏ includes a clear statement of areas of responsibility and authority
  ❏ spells out lines of reporting and control
  ❏ details the type and frequency of measures to monitor performance
  ❏ includes all the separate budgets for the major mix policy areas in a complete budget for the marketing function?

- Has the audit team asked the following five questions to assess the overall validity of the strategic marketing plan:
  ❏ By how much (if any) would the net profit contribution of the most profitable products be increased if there were an increase in specific marketing outlays, and how would such a change affect the strategy of competitors in terms of, say, market shares?
  ❏ By how much (if any) would the net losses of unprofitable products be reduced if there were some decrease in specific marketing outlays?
  ❏ By how much (if any) would the profit contribution of profitable products be affected by a change in the marketing effort applied to the unprofitable products, and vice versa, and what would be the effect on the total marketing system?

# THE STRATEGIC MARKETING PLAN AUDIT

❏ By how much (if any) would the total profit contribution be improved if some marketing effort were diverted to profitable territories or customer groups from unprofitable territorial and customer segments?

❏ By how much (if any) would the net profit contribution be increased if there were a change in the method of distribution to small unprofitable accounts or if these accounts were eliminated?

*Note*: These five questions are taken from Wilson's *Encyclopedia of Marketing* (1995).

*Having completed the administration and control sections of the marketing plan, the audit team should address communication and timing. Details of these two aspects of the plan are covered in Step 10 of Part 1. A few appropriate audit questions follow an outline of this step.*

## Step 10

# COMMUNICATION AND TIMING

### BACKGROUND INFORMATION

Lack of communication or miscommunication frequently cause business failures. A lack of communication when someone just forgets to pass on some information can be overcome with checklists, written plans and formal reporting systems. However, more difficult to solve is the situation where information does not exist because no one has identified the need for it and taken any steps to acquire it. The communication section of the strategic marketing plan is an ideal place to state clear policies for both gathering and disseminating information.

It is also important to include a single, consolidated timetable in this section containing all of the sequences and timings set out in previous sections of the marketing plan.

In the "Questions" section below you will find a set of audit questions dealing with communication and timing.

### QUESTIONS

- Does your communication section cover gaps in past information as well as the acquisition of new data needed for future plans?

- Does it also include a single, comprehensive timetable of all the sequences and timings set out in the preceding part of the plan?

- Have you drawn up a flowchart of the various stages of preparing the marketing plan and allocated a timescale to each one?

*Note*: An example of a marketing planning process timetable is provided in Table 8 in Part 1.

### CONCLUSION

Hopefully all of the questions listed in this section will help you by providing an overview of the factors to be covered by an effective strategic marketing plan and will allow you to assess the completeness and integrity of a formal plan. The detailed explanations in Part 1 will help you to answer these questions to best effect.

*Part 1*: **Michael J. Baker** *is Foundation Professor of Marketing at the University of Strathclyde. Following six years of industrial experience he took up a career in teaching and was sent to the Harvard Business School as a Foundation for Management Education Scholar. Appointed to the Faculty he taught the Creative Marketing Strategy course. At Strathclyde he has acted as Dean of the Business School, Chairman of the Graduate Business School, and Deputy Principal of the University (1984-91). The author/editor of over 30 books on marketing, he has served on the boards of numerous companies and worked with leading international firms such as Citibank, Dow, Honeywell, IBM and ICI.* **Part 2** *has been adapted from* The Company AuditGuide *published by Cambridge Strategy Publications Ltd.* **Part 3** *has been developed by Cambridge Strategy Publications Ltd.*